Six Steps

— *to* —

Six Figures

Release Your Fears, Own Your Worth,
and Ask for What You Want

SABIHA VORAJEE

BALBOA
PRESS
A DIVISION OF HAY HOUSE

Balboa Press books may be ordered through booksellers or by contacting:

Balboa Press
A Division of Hay House
1663 Liberty Drive
Bloomington, IN 47403
www.balboapress.com.au
1 (877) 407-4847

Print information available on the last page.

ISBN: 978-1-5043-0645-4 (sc)
ISBN: 978-1-5043-0646-1 (e)

Balboa Press rev. date: 03/13/2017

There comes a time when the risk to remain tight in the bud is more painful than the risk it takes to blossom.

—Anaïs Nin

For my Beloved.

CONTENTS

INTRODUCTION

What would it feel like to be able to *ask* for what you want to receive financially for the work you do? What if you asked in a way that used every aligned part of you—body, mind, heart, and spirit? What if your voice resonated with deep certainty and knowledge, and you just knew you were worth every cent you were asking for?

What would it be like to live, walk, talk, eat, sleep, work, and play in a body that tingles with vibrant, passionate energy, letting you know in every moment who you are and what you're capable of and that everything you choose is within your reach? You would simply have to have the courage, certainty, and confidence to ask for it.

What if, by owning the one thing that makes you feel like a woman (but has been negated and devalued in our society)—your powerful, feminine energy—is the one thing that can create the success, abundance, and fulfilment you want and dream of in a way that appears effortless and simple?

How would it be if you felt within the cells of your body, the marrow of your bones, the depths of your heart, that you were placed on this earth for a reason—to give your gifts and be rewarded handsomely for those gifts in every manner possible, especially financially?

What if you already had within you the confidence and certainty to ask for what you want, and all that's left is for you to own and claim what's rightfully yours—what you came to be, do, and have?

And in claiming your birthright, your inherent worthiness (which was never in doubt, but which you forgot in the tumultuousness of your life), you end up teaching, empowering, and leading other women to be and do the same?

Who would you be?

What would you do?

What would you create?

Whose lives would you touch and change?

Who would *you* become?

This book does not contain statistics, research, or studies on women about how we're still experiencing a pay gap, although this topic may come up. It's not a book about tricks of the trade; a vanilla, one-size-fits-all approach; or extra "stuff" you simply need to add to your already very full repertoire that allege to get you the success and money you want if you just do it the way they say you should.

This is not that kind of book. As much as those kinds of books can help us, in the end, all they really do is let us know how much we believe we still lack in being able to ask for and receive what we want and choose.

It's not that kind of book.

This is a book that will awaken within you questions from a body, mind, heart, and spirit perspective about why you may not be asking for what you want and will ultimately choose, and thereby not receiving what you desire. The reason I have written it in this way, is currently, with all the information we have at our fingertips, I still haven't come across a book that covers all the topics I'd like to discuss with you. Therefore, I have approached it in a way that encompasses all of who we are as women if we truly want success and abundance, material and otherwise, in our lives.

Asking for the money and wealth you want, or the promotions and opportunities that will allow you to live and give your gift from your heart and spirit requires us to start from deep within and not simply from the physical and mental faculties we rely on so heavily on a day-to-day basis.

It is my fervent desire for this book to show you how to be and do this, and I promise to provide start-to-finish spiritual, strategic, and practical strategies (gained from my many years of experience as a Human Resources professional from the other side of the interviewing table) that you can learn and apply and be the creator of all you choose.

In the being of this woman, know you have the power to ask for and receive exactly what you want.

This book is your roadmap to owning and claiming your magnificence. It becomes who you are and where you rarely question or doubt whether you're worth the money (or whatever else you'd like in your life) when you ask for it, even before you ask.

As women, we very often place ourselves last. We seem to believe that for us to be able to ask for what we want; first we must make sure everyone around us gets what they want. Until that happens, it's incredibly selfish to even imagine that we can ask for what we want.

We seem to believe we should give our gifts from the depths of our being and not ask for anything in return. After all, it's not very enlightened, spiritual, or feminine to ask for something in return for giving and living our gifts. Isn't this what we were born to do?

We seem to believe who we are and what we do should be seen, noted, and rewarded without our ever needing to say anything, because to ask for what we want isn't humble or gracious, and it's definitely not *feminine*.

We seem to believe we must prove our inherent worthiness in every waking moment about every aspect of our lives and in every role we play, because it can always be queried, doubted, or, God forbid, questioned, especially in our professional lives.

We seem to believe that for one of us to move ahead, one or more of us must fall and make way because there just isn't enough room at the top.

At some point, consciously or subconsciously, we give up or give in. We start playing the game the way we've been told we should play, because we believe we can't win any other way. Through this capitulation, we negate every voice within that is screaming at us to reclaim our magnificence, own our brilliance, and ask for what we deserve.

I grew up in a culture that told me being born a girl meant I wasn't to be seen or heard. For me to live my purpose, I was to abrogate all control to those who knew better and not question what I was told. I was lucky I had parents who truly believed in education for boys and girls, so my brother, sister, and I were educated to university level and went on to have successful careers in law, accountancy and Human Resources.

It was a given that as a boy, my brother would do this, but for my sister and I, it was considered arrogant to want an education. We didn't need to be educated, and we certainty didn't need to learn how to earn a living. Our husbands would do that for us.

I rebelled against everything I'd ever heard, determined to make my parents proud and shush the voices telling me that, as a woman, I was kidding myself that I would ever be successful.

I proved them wrong. In just under twenty years I had worked internationally in numerous large companies as an HR professional, specifically in the areas of reward and remuneration. From the bottom of the ladder to the top, I received salaries no one in my community could have told me I'd receive when I was a young woman, until eventually I retired from the industry, having reached the pinnacle I'd aspired to, started a new adventure and then returned, because I missed it.

But it wasn't without a price.

We've been told, to achieve what we truly desire, we must play by the rules–rules that, ironically, weren't created by us in the first place but which we must play by if we want to succeed.

Rules like be nice. Don't have too many opinions. Tone it down. Hide your femininity. Don't ask too many questions or challenge too many people. Be the peacemaker. Work much, much harder than anyone else. Don't you know you must work twice as hard to be half as good if you're a woman? Dress like a man, get a seat at the top table. Make sure you're heard. Don't worry about demonstrating your value— just keep endlessly proving your worth. Eventually, you'll get there.

I did get there, and for me my "there" was exactly what I wanted. However, I crashed and burned many times along the way. It was through these fortuitous crashes that I learned some invaluable lessons about how to be a highly successful, professional, feminine woman who could ask for the money, promotions, and opportunities I wanted and receive them.

Nonetheless, when I look back at my journey, I see all the advice I was given and took, and I concluded that most of it was completely counterintuitive. Being a woman, I took the much longer route to the joyful, authentic success I wanted to create.

I also realised most of it was piecemeal and not at all holistic, which, as a woman, had me feeling very one-dimensional for much of my professional life.

So, I asked myself a question and decided. What if I wrote a book sharing how to be a highly successful and fulfilled, powerfully feminine woman who knows how to strategically manage her career and earning capacity, articulate her value with confidence, certainty, and charisma, and be able to ask for and receive what she wants whenever she wants?

Not a bad idea, I thought.

Sure, there are lots of books out there on similar topics, but there isn't one written by someone who's worked in remuneration and reward internationally; who knows the insider workings of how organisations manage their reward strategies; who's created those very same strategies and lived it all herself by asking for and receiving what she wants; and who, in the process, coached many others to do the same.

Great idea, I thought.

And then, guess what happened? A thought popped into my head. A harbinger of doom. The killer of all desires and dreams. The death knell to courage and bravery—to pretty much everything we ever choose: *Who the hell are you to write such a book?*

That was when I knew I *had* to write this book. No matter what it took.

It never ends. That insidious voice that tries to undermine our every dream and desire, snuff out every spark we ever imagine of ourselves doing something magnificent, audacious, and life-changing. That voice tells us we're a fool for even thinking it. That voice never goes away, and too often we hear it subconsciously, and because we don't catch it and take it to task, it seeps away our inspiration, our passion, and our purpose. Before we know it, our dreams are off in the distance, no longer visible to the eyes or heart.

It's time to change this. Not just for ourselves but for girls and women everywhere.

I don't know about you, but I'm tired of hearing about the pay gap. I'm tired of hearing how, across most industries, women globally earn less than men, have access to fewer opportunities, must fight for what they want, have to put up with awful mistreatment sometimes, and even when they feel like they've succeeded or are succeeding, must work that much harder than their male counterparts to maintain their success, never mind elevate it to the next level.

I'm tired of hearing about how girls outperform boys throughout their schooling years, yet as they progress through their careers, the gap widens at every point, and they never seem to make it up.

I'm tired in this day and age of having access to so much information, intelligence, and knowledge, yet feeling like no matter how much we know, we're not changing the nature of the game or the levelness of the playing field.

I believe the status quo needs to change, and I am willing to challenge it and help it change.

I believe women *and* men want it to change, and both are willing to help it change so we all benefit. Otherwise, we're simply creating a different model of the same thing.

I believe it's time.

I also believe it's time to reclaim our powerful, feminine magnificence from the core of our soul, and help other women be and do the same. It's time to end the games that separate us as women; turning on each other because we believe we must to succeed. It's time to step into the true potential of who we really are, individually and as a collective group. We have the power to create and nourish life within us. Can we even absorb the enormity of such a thing? Yet it is one of the most unspoken, undervalued aspects of us as women, and it needs to change for ourselves, our partners, and our children.

We women are the true messengers of the change, starting at an individual level, because it is only when we see we aren't living our magnificence, our dreams, that we're falling short of being the inspiration we aspire to be, and then we start the journey.

This journey may not be for every woman. Our journeys are personal, and this is a journey that calls you. Some will hear the call and heed it. Others will hear the call, but the sound will be soft, barely heard, and they will walk on by.

All of which is perfect.

I believe our lives are our own, and the song by which we dance to our lives is also our own.

I believe every single one of us came into this life with a purpose, one that transcends every aspect of our lives, and some of us, especially women in this current climate, came to heal, reconnect, and fall deeply into and in love with our magnificent, feminine power. That way we can become the women and leaders we aspire to be, do the work we came to do, and inspire the next generation to become even more. As powerful, feminine women.

I believe one way to do this is by knowing our inherent worthiness, feeling it to the extent we never question it, and living and sharing our gifts personally and professionally from this place. In understanding how much value we must add, we then in return expect to receive the rewards, especially financially, that we so richly deserve.

I also believe we all have a very complex relationship with money: what it is; what it means; what it says about us if we like it, want it, and have it; or what it says if we like it, want it, and *don't* have it. Ultimately, I believe it's not about the money; still, only by taking this journey can we know this at our core for ourselves and then truly understand the role of money in a way where it simply floods our lives.

And finally, I believe as women we simply want to *feel* the magnificence of ourselves when we live true to our being and our soul. This is when who you believe yourself to be on the inside shows up fully on the outside, and none can deny its truth. When we embrace our powerful feminine. When we give our gifts and are rewarded. When we see how others are inspired by our example—be they our partners, children, family, friends, or strangers. When we shine our light, and our radiance is blinding. This is when we live the lives we were meant to live.

This is why we are here, why we came to be, and why I am writing this book.

If you're still reading, then I have a hunch you may be one of those who will join me and go on the journey.

There is a voice within calling you.

You've heard it many times.

Sometimes you've listened. Sometimes you've ignored it. Sometimes it made sense. Other times you were sure you were schizophrenic, because there was no way you were even going to contemplate doing what the voice suggested. Quit your job and travel for a year. Take a sabbatical and write a book. Marry him. Run as fast as you can in the opposite direction. Move to Australia (that last one was mine nine years ago. I listened in spite of the fact that most people thought I was crazy!) Move to Edinburgh (that one is mine too from last year, and here I am. In Edinburgh. No one thought I was crazy this time. They know me too well!)

Whatever the message, this voice is insistent in a way that resonates at a soul level, and as much as you try, it's very hard to dismiss. Then again, when it comes to your professional life, sometimes this voice gets drowned out by some other voice.

This other voice is the one we hear the most, the loudest and most ardently. It often tells us how we constantly and consistently fall short in everything we do at home, at work, with our family and friends, in our social lives. With our bodies, hobbies, and spiritual or creative pursuits, nothing escapes this voice.

This feeling of falling short mars everything, resulting often in a dismal lack of fulfilment in every aspect of our lives, even when we succeed, because often the thing we were chasing wasn't truly what was driving or inspiring us. It's what we believe we ought to want, have, and experience.

This voice is the voice without—a voice outside you that deceives you and throws you off your course. Through this book, I want to help you create from a space of confidence and certainty the strategies that will give you the ability to ask for what you want. My innermost ambitious and soulful desire is to help you cultivate the voice within, because this is the seat of your power.

Dr. John F Demartini, in his book, 'Count Your Blessings: The

Healing Power of Gratitude' talks about how "when the voice and the vision on the inside is more profound, and more clear and loud than all opinions on the outside, you've begun to master your life."

This is the journey I invite you on. This is a journey that can transform your life as it has mine, to the extent that when you navigate this terrain, it has the power to surprise and delight, and in some circumstances, stop you in your tracks, as you make the decision to take a deeper and more thorough look to what treasures are there deep within you. Why? Because this is the journey to your authentic self, power, and voice. When you own it in its entire glory—the good, the bad, and sometimes the ugly—it will transform you, because it is you, and it's perfect. This is key.

In my career, when I was young and having grown up in an Indian culture (second generation Indian from the sub-continent), bargaining and negotiating was second nature. I was cheeky enough to believe I could get away with simply asking for what I wanted, and for a while it seemed to work.

Then I got better at what I did, and I learned to ask in a better way. In turn I began to receive more. The more I asked, the more I learned, and the more I received. Eventually, within my field I really began to understand why I was receiving what I asked for pretty much every time, and it was only through sharing with some of my astounded friends each time I was promoted or got a new job what was offered to me, that it finally dawned on me why others, especially women, weren't asking. Or if they were, why they weren't receiving.

This book is a culmination of what I have been learning, living, and sharing for the past twenty years. And ladies, this book is all about us. It's about how we can create a movement to help all of us who are desirous of owning our magnificent, feminine power, learning how to articulate the significant value we add in everything we do with our own compelling, authentic, and gorgeous voices, and asking for and receiving what we want throughout our careers.

It's about changing our financial lives—the lives we've been afraid to grab hold and take control of because we've been told we don't know what we're talking about—and shaping it how we want it.

It's about feeling utterly and damnably good within our skin and experiencing inside-out transformation, so when we articulate how good we are, no one questions it, least of all us. We can ask for what we want and feel even better at receiving it.

And lastly, it's about changing the way the world interacts with us as powerful, feminine women. It's time for us to own who we are so we can share our gifts with the world, be the leaders we came to be, and inspire the next generation to take the baton and become even more than we can dream of right now.

If this is you, then I say, "Welcome home, sister."

HOW THIS BOOK WORKS

I hope this book will become your companion to the journey of yourself, as you seek to ask for and receive what you want throughout your career. I want to help you pull back the curtains, expose the untruths, decide how you want to deal with them, and make a commitment to the discovery of who you really are, so you can live and love the life you dream of and receive the money you want.

A powerful, magnificent, feminine woman who knows her worth is priceless. She can articulate her value with charismatic confidence and compelling certainty, and she asks for and receives what she chooses.

This book is essentially a subtle roadmap. How you use it is entirely up to you. This map is the journey to uncovering your authentic self. It's structured in three parts, six steps, and fifty-five chapters to make it clear how this will work.

The three parts cover the following areas:

❖ releasing your fears;
❖ owning your worth; and
❖ asking for what you want.

Within each section are integral components of the *Six Steps to Six Figures* philosophy. Steps one to three will be covered in part 1. Steps four and five will be covered in part 2, and finally, step 6 will be covered in part 3. Each step will have numerous chapters discussing in detail each relevant piece of the puzzle.

At the end of each chapter, to help you on your journey, I have created exercises in an associated book called the *Six Steps to Six Figures Vision Book*, which you can download for free online and have an online and hard copy (if you choose to print it) by following this link: <u>www.highvaluewoman.org/sstsfvisionbook</u>,

There are meditations within the online vision book that you can read and record to hear in your own voice, or you can simply download an audio of the meditation through the website via the links that will be available to you at relevant points throughout this book.

*

This book asks something of you: to take a risk on yourself by starting the journey using baby steps. As your awareness, knowledge, and confidence builds, begin applying what you learn in the real world. This is what will create the unwavering certainty within yourself—that you *do* have the power to create whatsoever you choose.

There are women who have utilised the strategies I am sharing with you, who within a day of talking to their manager have landed their dream job simply because they took a risk and asked. There are women who have smashed through major blocks and begun living the lives they dream of, doing the work they choose and have a passion for, simply because they got the deepest clarity of what had been holding them back, and they experienced a core, inside-out transformation that changed everything.

Reading books is wonderful—it's my favourite hobby and has been since I was a little girl. Reading books, absorbing what they teach you, assimilating the teachings within you, and then applying them is even more rewarding and has the capacity to change your life forever.

Read the chapters, and if you so wish, utilise the free *Six Steps to Six Figures Vision Book* online. Keep a journal to record your journey, and if you'd like, share with me how it's going for you. I would love to hear from you. You can reach me at <u>sabiha@highvaluewoman.org</u>

I know this work has the power to create the inside-out transformation I talk about. If this is what you choose—if you choose the life of your dreams and the financial abundance that is your birthright—take the risk, have a go, and start the journey.

You'll be truly glad you did.

I can't wait to hear about your success and fulfilment.

PART ONE

~Release Your Fears~

'Ultimately we know deeply that the other side of every fear is freedom.'

Marilyn Ferguson

Step 1: Your Invisible Barrier— Hitting Your Glass Ceiling

The journey to wholeness, to being who we really are, creating and living lives we truly choose often begins when the life we live is not placing us on the path to receive what we want.

An awareness, usually with a degree of pain, reminds us we're not where we want to be, haven't created what we want to create for ourselves and our loved ones. When we hit that all-too-familiar obstacle or wall, we sit up, dazed, our head spinning, and we wonder, Is this it? Am I going to keep landing here? What is this?

Hitting that wall is the first step. The journey to this place, what came before you hit it, is what we will uncover in this step, and it is the place to start.

CHAPTER 1

Are You Asking?

I remember the first time I asked for what I wanted in my career. Interestingly, my request wasn't directed at anyone but myself. I had recently begun a new job with a very large, very successful American financial services company. It would become the best career move I ever made. It had been eighteen months since I had completed my accountancy and economics degree, and I was working as a personnel officer (it wasn't called HR in those days), and through an almost nonsensical conversation, my best friend asked me to join her in the company she worked for, because if she successfully referred me, she would receive three hundred pounds and be able to buy the shoes she was after. Thus, I landed a role as a credit analyst with a company I knew I would go places with.

This intuitive decision allowed me to make the above-referenced career request. It happened following a conversation with my new manager. When I joined his team, he asked what my aspirations were for my career.

"The sky is the limit," he said. If I was passionate, dedicated, and committed to myself and my work, I could scale whatever ladder I chose.

I was twenty-four and had had a taste of HR and liked it, although I was in a role completely different from what I had wanted. I was confused but very driven—full of burning ambition.

After my new manager posed that career question, I went home to my empty apartment in North Wales, where I had moved to be able to take this job. As I made dinner that night, I asked myself, *where do I want my career to go? Where can it go?* It hadn't occurred to me in my naiveté that I couldn't ask this of myself, so I simply did.

I had studied accountancy and economics. As much as I had enjoyed the subjects, I'd had no intention of going into finance. Working in HR had sparked my desire for working with people, which I loved. Was that my vocation? I had no idea. What I did know was this: I wanted to be successful. I wanted to become an expert in my field—someone people liked and respected, and I also wanted to receive a truly excellent salary.

I felt as though I had started well. My salary was already above the graduate salary being offered in the market, and I knew if I worked hard (which was never an issue, given the work ethic passed to me by my parents), I would receive the money I wanted and create the success I desired.

When I spoke to my manager at our next meeting, I let him know I was interested in pursuing a career in HR. I had anticipated his being disappointed in me, given I'd not even been in my role on his team for two months, and here I was, already planning on moving into another area.

That wasn't the case. He listened intently to why I was interested in HR, and after a few minutes of conversation, gave me names of people in HR he suggested I touch base with, letting them know of my interest and desire. There were always opportunities occurring within the organisation, and although there were policies regarding how and when one could apply for a role outside one's own department, my manager let me know it was possible.

I was willing to do what it took. Within six months I had moved into the payroll team in the company. Within six months of that move, I was selected to be part of an organisation-wide business internship program. This was a bank initiative that ran for six months, with all ten interns rotating through every department in the bank. We experienced amazing opportunities and ended with positions best suited to our attitudes and attributes. I ended up moving to Ireland to head up the payroll area. Within two years of that move, I was the most senior compensation, benefits, and payroll person, heading up the function for the Irish subsidiary. I was twenty-nine years old and had achieved my dream job in four short years.

I learned to ask, and throughout my career I never stopped asking. Maybe it was due to my Indian background. Coming from a patriarchal community that didn't believe in educating women (my parents were ahead of their time), I learned that in order to receive what I wanted, I had to ask—and on occasion fight for it. I've always been passionate, so finding a way to get what I wanted was never an issue. As strategy after strategy worked, I simply kept asking and receiving.

It struck me as fascinating when I started seeing within my own career in remuneration and reward how there was a constant and continuing gap between what men and women earned. It seemed that very few women would actually *ask* for the money, the promotion, or the opportunity they wanted. This isn't to say women don't ever ask. In my experience, the disparity I noticed was they simply don't ask as often as men do, and not to the extent men do. This may seem like a trite remark, but it isn't. Every choice we make, irrespective of the circumstances surrounding the choice, is our decision.

In just under twenty plus years of my career, I have watched, analysed, worked with, reported on, presented to, created numerous strategies, papers, initiatives, and solutions on and regarding this phenomenon. Where relevant, I have talked to and coached men and women when it came to bettering their chances of receiving the money, promotions, or opportunities they wanted. One thing stands out above all others. When it comes to *asking* for money, promotions, or opportunities, more than 75 percent of my conversations with employees have been with men.

In the last ten years of my career, as I became good at asking for what I wanted, I began asking women around me why they weren't asking. What astounded me the most was that many seemed surprised by my question. It hadn't occurred to them to ask. Many said they weren't sure how. Some didn't think it was appropriate. Others pointed out their companies had remuneration strategies and annual review programs, and they worked within those boundaries. Some felt they didn't need to ask because they didn't imagine they were underpaid—a notion they often realised to be incorrect after further discussion with me. Some of the women didn't like talking about money. Some were offended I had even asked. Some flinched and said it wasn't important—although their body language told me the opposite. In the end, after unceasingly studying the topic, I realised this subject at its core was much, much bigger than I had ever imagined.

The pay gap is an issue. In this day and age, it's embarrassing that we still have women who are paid less than men, and even more so, for doing the same or similar work. Without getting into this too deeply (there are so many reasons and opinions as to why this exists), one thing is clear. Women want to receive what they believe they deserve, but far too often they believe they are already being paid so and that the next pay raise, promotion, or opportunity will happen when it's time, and they will be asked about or notified of it.

When I ask women, "When was the last time you asked for a pay raise, a promotion, or an opportunity you really wanted?" they often reply they want to do so. In some circumstances, they have even gone as far as getting it, but it's always as if it's happened by magic, as a coincidence, or by happenstance. *Luck* is a word I hear often. What makes me smile is these are women I see as leaders in their industries, yet when it comes to asking for what they want, they tell me they feel like they fall short far too often.

When I share some of my experiences as a head of reward, about how often the opportunities that come up are snapped up before they're even on paper, they're often surprised. I share that this is usually because someone has created an opportunity either by simply asking about it (as I have done in the past) or by putting his hand up for it before it was even officially available. When I explain this, the lightbulb moment occurs. Women realise the promotions and opportunities they are waiting for are being given to others (often to men, because they've asked for them) before qualified women even show up. This is not always the case, but it is a common occurrence (and even more frequent as one goes further up the corporate ladder). Therefore, asking for what you want before you're completely ready for it is critical.

Therefore, I ask you, "Are you asking?" If you are, good for you, and I hope you're getting the results you want. I hope this book helps you to ask and receive even more.

If you're not, why not?

I have a firm belief in the work I do. Asking for money, promotions, and opportunities we want isn't simply about asking for and receiving what we deserve. It's about owning our inherent worth, putting it out into the world for the betterment of everyone, and knowing that when we live and give our glorious gifts, the universe rewards us. One of the ways this occurs is through money.

When we're not living this, it's because something is stopping us. Releasing our fears is the first part of this journey. Owning our intrinsic worth is the next, and that's about much more than receiving money. Being able to articulate this from a place of authentic confidence, profound certainty, and our own powerful charisma from a place of true win-win is the final step.

This is what I hope to share with you in this book: to not only help you get what you want but to help your organisation get what it wants too, and to start eliminating the pay gap.

I believe it's time to change the story and create a new legacy, one of financial education and empowerment for girls and women everywhere. It's a mission and vision I believe worth living for.

I hope you're with me.

If you'd like to journal your journey using the *Six Steps to Six Figures Vision Book* and access the exercise pertaining to this chapter, please visit www.highvaluewoman.org/sstsfvisionbook and submit your details. You will be given immediate access. Enjoy!

CHAPTER 2

What Happens When We Don't Ask?

Economist Linda Babcock of Carnegie Mellon University and co-author with Sara Laschever of *Women Don't Ask* and *Ask for It* has stated that women often leave between $1 million to $1.5 million dollars on the table when they don't ask for the money they want.

Across the globe, millions of women will earn less than their male counterparts for the work they do and often, for doing same or similar work.

- In the United Kingdom and United States, women will earn £500,000 and $1.2 million, respectively, less than men.
- In Australia, the average twenty-five-year-old male will earn $2.4 million over the next forty years, compared to $1.5 million an average female will earn.
- Women are two and a half times more likely to live in poverty in their old age than men.
- By 2019, the average woman will have half the amount of pension/401K/superannuation than a man has.
- Men with children earn almost double what women with children earn over their lifetime.

These are some potential financial consequences women face when they don't ask for what they want, and they can be substantial.

What is even more significant and concerning from a broader holistic perspective is the emotional and spiritual impact it has on us as women, when we're either struggling financially or simply have a feeling we could be doing better in the money and wealth stakes. When we inherently know we could be doing better financially and aren't, due to the subconscious, innate discrimination prevalent in a system that only fifty years ago deemed it was okay to pay women less than men. The impact this has on us about how we feel about ourselves on all levels can be devastating.

The global domain in which all of this is going on is having an impact on girls and women everywhere, about all aspects of us, our place in the world, and our ability to make it what we want to be. It also determines how we move forward in life. We hear relentlessly about the pay gap yet still watch as male leaders within our biggest organisations don't implement real solutions and make them work. It's frustrating to know that as a woman my skills and abilities may be priced subconsciously at a reduced rate simply because of my gender. All these things and more contribute to an overall sentiment for women of feeling undervalued, unworthy, and undeserving not only of asking for what we want but receiving it.

Our seemingly inherent and subconscious lack of belief in who we are as women is the core issue and challenge, and when we can readily embody the truth that is our power and pass it onto the next generation, who can aim to soar even higher than we might dream, then we have at one level fulfilled what we came here to be and do. Pave the way for the next generation.

At a collective subconscious level, until we can all let go of the unequal past where we have had to fight for our very survival, the survival of our children, and most importantly our voice and who we are at our core—a powerful manifestation of the divine feminine—until we find ways of letting go of this, personally and as a community and society, we will not create the kind of passionate, joyful, abundant, and downright wealthy life we want and deserve. The kind of life where everyone wins, not just the tiniest, white male minority.

I grew up in a very patriarchal culture and watched as women lost their voices or lived lives without one from the start, struggling financially because the rules had forbidden them to act to take care of themselves and their families without having to be entirely dependent on others. This created within me a deep desire to make it better not only for myself but for all women.

It pains me to see women run themselves into the ground, trying to be and do everything for everyone, and put themselves last every time, from the big things to the smallest. When the tiniest moments of joy can't be accessed until everyone else has had theirs, and it's hard to even remember what our moments of joy are.

When we don't ask for what we want, it negates who we are from within the deepest part of us, and bit by bit we slowly erode any advance we may have made at any level. Individually and personally, we live a life of constantly chasing our tail, feeling and being "not enough" in anything, and always having a niggling sense of somehow being left behind, of not having a clue how it happened. Or maybe feeling like it's always been that way.

Throughout my work and life, I haven't experienced many women who, when asked about how they feel about themselves, have been able to answer that they love themselves and everything in their lives unconditionally and that every moment is a joy.

For us to feel this way, we often imagine every aspect of our life must be perfect, yet we know in our cells this will never be the case. Perfection doesn't exist, yet we still chase it physically, mentally, emotionally, and spiritually. Logically we know we're chasing a will-o'-the-wisp, yet we can't seem to stop.

Why? And how does this tie into the concept of not asking and its impact?

When we don't believe deeply in ourselves, who we are and what we do; when we believe we must fight for everything we want; when our experience is that for us to get what we want; we must be the opposite of who we are, then we hold back from asking for what we want and being able to receive it.

Or if we do ask, we ask from a place of entitlement or demand or worse: a complete lack of worthiness. These spaces may give us what we want, but at a cost that hurts us more than the one doing the giving.

So, what is the ultimate impact of not asking, or of asking from a place of not being in alignment with who we truly are?

At an individual and personal level, we manifest an endless cycle of "not-enoughness"—of struggle, lack, and scarcity, and ultimately, a compounding effect of the belief already within us of, "I'm not worth it." We listen ardently to the voices outside, forgetting we have a much stronger voice within, and we wonder why we feel empty, no matter how hard we work or how successful we become.

At a community level, we strengthen all the above, and we live it and teach it to each other subconsciously. In being able to empathise and sympathise with our common not-enoughness, we create connection and continue to perpetuate the myth, ensuring we keep it in place for our daughters, granddaughters, and nieces and generations to come.

At a societal level, we maintain the status quo. Change is slow, inconsistent, and doesn't last. We find ourselves taking two steps forward and three steps backward. We allow the myths to run our lives; the voices outside are so very loud; and because we don't own our enoughness, our worthiness, in the end our hamster wheel runs faster and faster, and we become emptier and emptier to the point where our power drains away at an exponential level.

We lose our connection to the collective divine feminine power. The part of us that is connected to each other and all that is. We grieve silently in the darkness of our heart and soul, wondering who and what we are crying for.

Not asking can equal experiencing unworthiness at our core. In every aspect of our life, not just professionally, when we don't ask for what is inherently ours, what we came to claim and own and then to give back to an even greater degree, everyone loses.

I've talked a lot above about the bigger picture of not asking, but the tragedy of not asking always starts with us, as individuals. We experience much of the above, and because everyone is living it, it makes it even harder to imagine it being any different.

Well, it can be different, and as with everything in life, it all starts with a choice. The choice of understanding that asking for what you need and want is not a reflection of your worthiness; it is your birthright, just as it's seen as a birthright for everyone who does ask. It doesn't require you to be at the end of the list. Deciding you have every right to ask, and the other has every right to say no, is simply part and parcel of the journey.

In that case, why have we forgotten how to ask, and how can we make it simply a part of who we are from now on?

We will talk about this a lot more later, but for now, as we continue unlocking the doors to why we don't ask or haven't been asking, take a little time to complete the exercise if you'd like in the online vision book (see link below) and reflect on what it means for you, your life, and the people in it when you don't ask.

If you'd like to journal your journey using the *Six Steps to Six Figures Vision Book* and access the exercise pertaining to this chapter, please visit www.highvaluewoman.org/sstsfvisionbook and submit your details. You will be given immediate access. Enjoy!

CHAPTER 3

Why Aren't You Asking?

If you answered at the end of chapter 1 that you haven't been asking for either the money you want, the promotion you've wanted for a while, or the new opportunity that will take you to the next level in your career, I'm curious: Why aren't you asking?

In a little while we'll discuss why you may not have been asking, in the hope that we can begin changing the old paradigm and commence constructing a new one, one that has the potential in you receiving what you want, giving you the courage and conviction to really start asking for everything you want, when you want it, for the rest of your life.

There are many reasons why women aren't asking, but at the end of the day, the only one that matters is the one that's relevant to you, if you want to ask for what you feel you deserve and so far, haven't. This is because all else pales in comparison to what is true in your life. The research, studies, books, papers—all the information as to why women aren't asking—isn't going to change the ultimate outcome now of the challenge you may currently have of wanting something and not feeling able to ask for it.

Asking for what we want has always struck me as a bit of an enigma. After all, when we were young children we didn't shy away from asking for what we wanted. As babies, we were quite happy to let our needs and wants be known, and we certainly didn't hold back in asking. Often, we received it, and no one made us feel as if we were "less than" because we asked.

The point here is, when did we learn, especially as women, that we couldn't ask for what we wanted, and if we did ask, it was seen as something less than?

When did asking for what we wanted start to be seen as weak? What changed within us and our society that we decided we had to find a way of making it all happen ourselves, and it had to happen for others before it happened for us?

This new way of being, of seeing ourselves as more, began when, through the world wars, women were asked to step into work outside the home, and we began accessing, utilising, and demonstrating our abilities and power. We always knew we were more; we'd simply been denied the opportunities. But now we were needed, and we realised we could be much more than we had been allowed to be.

Yet instead of it empowering us and showing us all we could be and continuing to grow holistically in this space, somehow it became our prison as we became responsible for everything, to the deep detriment and cost of ourselves. We went from a culture that had us as mistresses of the home to one where we were given "suitable" work outside the home, and within the space of sixty years created such significant leaps and bounds we could never have imagined. Yet during it all, we took on the mantle of needing to prove our worth to be considered worthy and suddenly asking for anything implied unable or unworthy.

Worthiness is a huge topic and will be covered throughout this book, but I'd like to make a mention of this here to set the scene for you. The ability to ask, I believe, comes from a place of deep worthiness; of knowing, believing, and experiencing on a regular basis our own sense of who we are and why we're here. The very fact we're alive and breathing creates magic we can't even begin to fathom. When we live from this space, asking for what we need and want solidifies our worthiness more and more, and in the end, we live in a space of grace and ease because we know we're unique and worthy, and it can never be questioned. It resonates at an energetic level; it's challenging to say no to, and it is this space where I will show you how to cultivate in your life, so that asking becomes as natural as breathing.

The power to ask is also strengthened once we know who we truly are, why we're here, and what we're meant to do, and it is this passion we bring to our work, vocation, and career. These are the irresistible and compelling people we love to admire and be inspired by, and there isn't one of them who doesn't have a burning desire for what they do. We also all know burning desires can burn, and it can be this subconscious fear of "burning up" that can stop us in our tracks and cease all notion of even considering asking for what we want.

The burning desire behind my asking for what I wanted was a dream I had, coming from the background of wanting to change the possibilities open to women in my culture. I watched as many women struggled to cope when traditional models they had been raised with fell to the wayside, leaving them in dire financial and social circumstances, sometimes ostracised, sometimes bereft of any kind of support if they chose an alternative lifestyle to the one that had been deemed suitable for them.

All of this made me determined to change the way women saw themselves, to understand the true nature of their power and the real impact they could have, if they simply chose their destiny, rather than allowing others to choose it for them.

Whenever I imagined what it would take for me to create this change, my first thought was always, *Oh boy, maybe it's too big.*

Then I would imagine the faces of the people around me as I attempted to do what I said I would. The thought in my mind then would be, *You're crazy. Who the hell do you think you are, imagining you can do this? You can't change generations of history.*

Not the most helpful thoughts, I agree. However, I have a stubborn and contrary streak, and when I heard these thoughts, my passion to end the pain I know these women were in or had been in (similar to some of my own experiences) made me learn to pay little or no attention to them, and I continued my way.

Further along the journey, more thoughts came in response to what I suppose could be classed as failures. *You're not cut out for this. You're kidding yourself. Seriously, this is too big for you. You can't do this.*

Yet once again, I kept going.

Throughout this, I learned how difficult it was to go against the grain. This can be one of the most frightening experiences one can have, whether it's a traditional, patriarchal culture; family norms; the unspoken agreements at a social level between friends and loved ones; the rules and policies within an organisation; or your own thoughts and beliefs (to make a stand is to put yourself outside your comfort zone).

It is also the main reason we hold back from asking for what we want, taking a risk, and following our dreams. The potential for it to backfire in our face, lose connections of family and friends, and miss out on the very things we want can happen, yet often it's the mere thought of them that stops us, not the reality that may or may not be.

This is the beginning of the journey where we will look at, what is this for you? It may be one big one, numerous small ones, or a mixture of both. In any event, it's time to decide and choose a path.

If you'd like to journal your journey using the *Six Steps to Six Figures Vision Book* and access the exercise pertaining to this chapter, please visit www.highvaluewoman.org/sstsfvisionbook and submit your details. You will be given immediate access. Enjoy!

CHAPTER 4

Asking for What You Want: A Must, or Nice to Have?

One of the biggest a-ha moments I've ever had was when I ran one of the first half-day workshop sessions in my business. I had a roomful of women who had given up their Saturday morning to come hear about how they could begin their journey of *Six Steps to Six Figures.*

It was a very exciting morning for me: sharing my content; coaching within the sessions; listening to these beautiful women open their minds and hearts and share what was going on for them; and as we got toward the end of the session, one of the participants made a comment that truly made me stop and later ponder and reflect deeply on what she had said.

I had asked the women to share one thing they had received from the session, and this comment opened not only my eyes but the eyes of all the other women as they nodded in agreement.

The comment this lovely woman shared was, "Listening to what we've talked about this morning, I realise the reason I haven't been asking for what I want is simply because for me, it seemed like a nice to have, rather than a must."

My jaw dropped. I'm not sure how many others did as well. We continued the conversation, finally ending the session, yet her words stayed with me.

Asking for what she wanted was a nice to have, not a must.

There were many questions running around in my mind as I

ruminated on her comment. Asking for what she wanted was a nice to have, not a must. In that case, did she believe she was already receiving what she wanted, and was this due to being based on the role she did? Was she financially secure in a way that any extra money was a bonus rather than a necessity? Why was money a nice to have for her, rather than a must? Did many women see money this way?

The questions were numerous, and of course, no answers were forthcoming.

Why? Because this is a question we must answer for ourselves.

I can sit here and say, "Asking for what you want has to be a must; otherwise you won't be and do what it takes," but to be honest, throughout my career I never considered it in such a way.

For me, asking for what I wanted was part of the journey to my next promotion and/or opportunity, and I was determined I would receive what I wanted. Not only because I had financial targets I wanted to achieve in my life, but because I knew receiving the money would assist me in an ongoing basis on valuing myself, my skills, and my abilities, and the more I focused on the money, the more I would find ways of articulating the value I would add to the people and organisations I was pitching to.

My focus became, "How can I let them see how it's a win-win for them to pay me what I'm asking and for me to receive it?"

This made the concept relatively simple, and money was purely part of the equation when it came to promotions and opportunities. Working in the field of reward and remuneration also put money at the forefront of my mind, which helped.

Going back to the concept of "asking for what you want is a nice to have, rather than a must" is a notion you must decide for yourself.

The subject of money and our relationship with it and to it is one we will cover a little later in the book. It holds a large part of the key as to why we behave the way we do when it comes to the subject, and it's our conscious and subconscious beliefs about money and how it relates to us that govern how we then interact with it in all aspects of our lives.

The bottom line for the idea we're talking about here is this. If you decide, based on your beliefs, that money as a part of your career is a nice to have, then it will be low or lower down on your list of what is important to you, and you may or may not ask for what you want. This is your choice. If money is as important to you as the promotion and/ or opportunity, then the likelihood is you will ask for it, and you will find ways of asking for it that work for you and for the people you're asking as much as possible.

The upside of this is if you ask, it's far more likely you will receive, and you will get better at asking. Your relationship with money—how to manage it, work with it, ask for it, and utilise it and articulate your request for it—will deepen until you realise the ultimate truth: it was never about the money in the first place.

Taking this journey is transformational, because most of the baggage we hold as to why we're not asking comes from this space of our relationship to money and subsequently to who we believe ourselves and money to be. Taking this journey means poking in the corners of our beliefs and thoughts until we uncover all that doesn't serve us, and replace it with what does. Taking this journey means a deep awareness of your true nature and identity and an ability to become an alchemist when it comes to money, so in the end, as well as asking for the money you want, you begin to attract it to you.

This is the destination and then the beginning of a new journey.

But I'm getting ahead of myself. This is what is open to you if you decide money is a must or a want, rather than a nice to have.

As with all the information in this book, it's your choice.

If you'd like to journal your journey using the *Six Steps to Six Figures Vision Book* and access the exercise pertaining to this chapter, please visit www.highvaluewoman.org/sstsfvisionbook and submit your details. You will be given immediate access. Enjoy!

CHAPTER 5

The truth about Worth and Value

One of the most fascinating concepts I've ever come across within this subject is about the notion of worth versus value.

The first time I pondered this subject, I felt somewhat uneasy. It was a subconscious misgiving, and it took me a while to figure out why I was experiencing such a disturbance within myself about it.

What was making me feel restless was the idea that someone could ever pay me what I'm worth. This was because deep within, I've somehow always held the belief that I am priceless as a human being. There will never be a price that could ever articulate the value of a human soul, and so for someone to try to pay me what I'm worth was, in fact, a nonsensical idea.

What made complete sense was the idea that someone could place a value (pound, dollar or otherwise) on the value I created (again, pound, dollar or otherwise). My background in accountancy worked well for me in my career within reward and remuneration, because as a reward professional creating strategies for the organisations I worked in, the main driver was productivity and performance and how well it could be measured. This thereby allowed us to know and calculate a potential return on the investment we were making for our people.

One of the challenges of working in Human Resources is the age-old test of articulating the value, and more importantly the return on investment (ROI) of the workforce. People are often an organisation's biggest asset (if managed effectively and efficiently) and its biggest cost (usually a given.) In no other area is there more friction than in the battle of utilising one's workforce, so they are creating and adding value and helping to grow the business, not simply being an overhead cost.

Within my field and work, my task was to come up with ways to help the organisation improve productivity, better manage performance, and of course create reward strategies that would satisfy our people, ultimately creating an ROI we were making of them in the first place. Trying to articulate a start to end return on investment on an individual is a challenging task, unless you're in a revenue-generating area, and even then, there may not always be a clean or clear line of sight from the work to the outcome.

Therefore, reward has always been about the investment an organisation makes strategically with the intention of growing the business, or adding value to the extent there is a positive ROI on the money it has already spent, especially of its people. Figuring out early in my career how I could communicate an ROI for a pay raise, promotion, or opportunity I wanted was one of the biggest lessons I ever learned, and throughout my career I became good at it. I have a naturally inquisitive mind when it comes to finance, people, and how the two interact, and in my field, I learned how to speak the language that would help me get ahead, help my manager in his or her role, move our department forward, and ultimately be a success for the business as a whole.

Managing my career in this way became a strategic imperative, and as my career grew, so did my remuneration, to the point where I ceased being a permanent member of staff and became a contractor. It gave me the flexibility and the ability to receive what I chose, and on occasion I made the decision to become permanent again, if the opportunity merited it, which it often did.

I learned I could always find a way of communicating and articulating the value I was adding to the organisation, because my work inclined me to do so. It also built a solid sense of myself, my skills, my abilities, and my experiences, and having started my career in what felt like a meritocracy (I now understand the truth of that myth), I took the idea to heart. It was also what was required me of when I was on the other side of the interviewing table—helping my managers manage their reward strategies and budgets and ensuring they played the game of remuneration with their teams within the scope of the policies set by the company.

Helping people approach salary conversations and assisting managers to have better salary discussions, ensuring a win-win, became my mantra, and it was one that I saw reap significant rewards for myself, the individuals, managers, and organisations concerned.

It all came from the notion that one can never ask for what one's worth: one, because it's impossible (we're priceless), and two, because you can't articulate it in a way that makes any kind of commercial sense.

What we can do, however, is learn how to speak the language of commercial value from an individual and role perspective, tied to what the organisation is trying to create and articulate it in this way, with our own special brand of charisma. This isn't easy, but it is simple and can be done, and once you know how to do it, it becomes an ingrained strategy that can reap significant financial and other rewards for the rest of your life.

It can also change the inner trajectory of your life, and this then becomes the true reason to ask for what you want. Not just because you want to receive the money, but because now you know how to ask from a place of deep worthiness. This is the goal. It is no longer about the money, and you realise it never was.

Therefore no one will ever pay you what you're worth, but they can pay you for the significant value you add through who you are, what you bring to the table in terms of skills, abilities, and experience, and what you are demonstrating you will create for all concerned.

This is why, when I hear women talk about proving their worth, rather than what I hear men say, which is "demonstrating their value," it makes me pause and ask myself, "Why do women believe they have to constantly prove their worth when men believe they simply have to articulate and demonstrate their value?"

I believe it is due to the fact that we as women live in a patriarchal, "false-masculine" world, where the model of success is masculine, and where collectively, we have not yet accessed and owned our inherent feminine power and are living it with every part of ourselves in a way that is deeply successful *and* emotionally fulfilling.

We live in a world where the noise outside of us is so loud, we can't hear ourselves or allow ourselves to simply be.

When was the last time you paused, took the deepest breath in, looked around your world and everything in it, and simply gave thanks for it without thinking it needed to be different?

We feel the need to prove our worth when within our deepest core, we don't believe ourselves to be enough physically, mentally, emotionally, and spiritually. Each time we compare ourselves to another and we find ourselves wanting, we deepen the "not-enoughness" of us, and we dig that hole deeper. Our inherent worthiness slips away just a bit more.

Each time we imagine another woman to be more beautiful, sexy, or gorgeous; anytime we imagine she is more intelligent, scintillating, or charismatic; or loving, nurturing, or kind—whatever it may be—if you compare yourself against another and find yourself wanting, the darkness becomes just a bit darker, the fear a tad more intense, and you wonder when it will all crash around you and the world will finally discover what a fraud you are.

This is why we as women feel we must prove our worth time and time again. It is a topic that is very dear to my heart, because I believe it is the biggest lie we have ever told been told and one we continue to tell ourselves without even realising it.

When we never allow ourselves to imagine that maybe, just maybe, since there's no one out there at all like me, they don't even have my DNA, maybe all this comparing is a useless waste of energy?

Making the decision to own *your* magnificent worthiness, to know it deeply and own it in this crazy, crazy world takes time, but it is very possible, and it's my invitation as we go through this book that you decide this is the ultimate journey and the real reason you're reading this book.

This is the strategy that becomes yours and allows you to scale the ladders you choose to scale, because no one else can. This is the strategy that will let you know once and for all—

You have no true competition. Ever.

If you get this, it will change everything for you. Everything.

If you'd like to journal your journey using the *Six Steps to Six Figures Vision Book* and access the exercise pertaining to this chapter, please visit www.highvaluewoman.org/sstsfvisionbook and submit your details. You will be given immediate access. Enjoy!

CHAPTER 6

What's Getting in Your Way? Realising You Have a Glass Ceiling

We all stop at times.

This is normal and simply a part of life. We hit a dead end. Something finishes. Someone decides and an ending comes about. These make up a part of our lives, and we find a way to move on and move forward. It can be immediate or after a period of time. But in the end, we all move on.

When we find ourselves running into the same obstacle, or the same or a similar situation, the outcome seems to be the same as well. Maybe it's a different obstacle or situation, but deep down you have a feeling that it's the same; it just looks different.

When we end up in this situation, we have a sinking feeling in the pit of our tummy, a disquieting restlessness covers us, and we find ourselves saying, "Oh, I can't believe this happened to me." Or, "I can't believe it's happened again." Or, "Why me? Seriously—again? Doesn't all the work I've done count for anything?" When we reach this point time and time again, a moment is upon us. And it's not the moment you think it is.

It is a moment of eventuality and possibility. Eventuality in the sense of finality, and we pause long enough to have a conscious spark of recognition. A thought of, *Oh, I've been here before, and maybe this is the last time I want to be here.* Possibility, because once the spark has fought its way to the forefront of our consciousness, now we're aware of it, and a desire is born. It may be a simmering desire rather than a burning one, but it's the flame that has been lit, and no matter how much we try, we can't go back.

This is the time, when if we choose conscious awareness and our passion is also stirred, we subconsciously (or sometimes consciously) make the decision for it to be different, and in doing so, we realise we're hitting the same barrier and have been for some time. The same thing is getting in our way, again and again, and it's stopping us.

This is the time of choice.

It is a time when possibility and potential are stirred within us, plus frustration, anger, and several other emotions as we tangle with the fact we've been here time and time again and now we really mean it. No more!

If, throughout your life, you've ever found yourself saying or experiencing any of the above, then you are, as so many of us have experienced, hitting an invisible barrier—your very own glass ceiling.

Now, the concept of a glass ceiling is a familiar one for all women, but it's always been a generic one, and not one we've ever truly be able to relate to, and because we can't relate to it due to its non-specificity, we tend to dismiss it, even though it's a huge issue in our society.

I find it fascinating when I talk to some women and they tell me they haven't really experienced a glass ceiling—therefore, they're not sure it exists. Yet when I dig deeper, inevitably there is always something we experience at some level that is stopping us from being who we want to be, doing what we want to do, and having what we want to have. And of course, it's rare that I meet a woman who is receiving the money she wants.

Consequently, no matter how little you may feel you're experiencing a glass ceiling, the likelihood is at some level you are. If you don't have the life you truly want, you're hitting *your* glass ceiling. We all are, and it's ours. Not anyone else's, and recognising it is the first and most important step.

Congratulations! It's time to celebrate!

Now, before you think I've lost the plot and you put this book down to get yourself a stiff drink, or a glass of wine, or something equally intoxicating, please bear with me. Most people live lives of quiet desperation, as Henry David Thoreau once quoted so eloquently (and rather sadly, I believe). A life filled with a sense of there being something more, but you just can't see it, and because you can't, or you never do, life passes you by, and as Dr Wayne Dyer said in his book, "10 Secrets for Success and Inner Peace," 'you die with your music still inside you'.

This to me is a tragedy, and it's a tragedy because it's one that can be averted by a simple act of awareness and choice.

Traditionally, the glass ceiling as a metaphor has been used to describe the invisible barriers through which women can see what they want but can't reach them. I like this definition, however, and for the purposes of this book and my work, I use the "glass" in the glass ceiling to represent a lack of awareness of our own personal invisible barriers. These are the ones we hit time and time again, and we seem to keep hitting them because we can't *see* them. We can see what we want—we just can't get past our own "stuff." Our barriers are transparent, invisible to a large extent, so we bash our noses and wonder why.

If you're constantly coming up against the same obstacle, the same situation, or the same outcome repeatedly, and you can't seem to get past it, then this is *your* glass ceiling. It's time to stop hitting our noses on the glass, turning around and then running back at it again, fiercer and more determined than ever, only to hit it even harder the next time, and come away with an even bloodier nose!

What if, instead, the next time you hit that invisible barrier, rather than turning around and going at it again, you made the decision to strategically stop and look at the barrier?

What if you took the time to look at what is making you hit the barrier again?

What if this time you studied the barrier, looked at it from every angle, analysed your part in the barrier being there, and asked yourself, "How am I keeping this barrier up?"

What if you realised this barrier and your hitting it was not an obstacle but a signpost?

What if this barrier was trying to send you a message?

What if the message of the barrier was, "Hey, I'm still here. Who you're being, what you're doing isn't working, and I hate to say this, but every time you run at me, even if you've made a change somewhere, it's not working because you haven't addressed the core issue."

If this was the message of your invisible barrier and you chose to listen it to it and listen to the real message it's giving you, would it still feel like a barrier and an uphill struggle?

Or would it feel like you were finally waking up, and maybe choosing to look at what's really going on?

When we keep coming up against the same barriers, the same responses, situations, or outcomes, it doesn't matter how much work we may have already done. The fact we're still experiencing the same outcomes means we haven't got to the bottom of it.

The root cause.

The core issue.

This is what inside out transformation is about. Getting to the heart and soul of the matter, the things that are blind to us, which we must now find the courage to face if we want to feel, know, and experience the truth of who we are and why we are experiencing what we have been, good or bad.

This is where, if you make the decision to look deeper, you start to see how the pieces in the puzzle may or may not be what you thought they were.

There is a scene in one of my favourite films, *Interview with the Vampire*, starring Tom Cruise and Brad Pitt, where once Brad's character has made the decision to end his life and become a vampire, he takes some time to look at the things he will never see again. For example, how his garden appears to him as a human being. A sunrise. He watches as the sun rises above the horizon for the last time for him, and then he turns and goes through the process of becoming a vampire.

The minute his pain ends and he has transformed into a vampire, he begins walking around his garden once again, seeing all the things he has seen countless times before, only now they are very different. My favourite is the statue of the angel whose eyes now follow his every move.

Pausing to truly look at what is causing you to hit your barrier, your glass ceiling, from a root perspective, wanting to know once and for all what the core issue is—this is the start of the transformation this journey can create for you, and women who have already been through it marvel at how "blind" they felt prior to it.

This is the game, and it is a game in which you will scream in horror and squeal in delight, similar to being on a crazy ride at a theme park. I've always loved roller coasters. I was never a big fan of the merry-go-round. I found it a tad boring.

So saying, how ready are you to ride?

If you'd like to journal your journey using the *Six Steps to Six Figures Vision Book* and access the exercise pertaining to this chapter, please visit www.highvaluewoman.org/sstsfvisionbook and submit your details. You will be given immediate access. Enjoy!

CHAPTER 7

Triggers—the Keys to Awareness and Consciousness

Knowing you have your own glass ceiling, as mentioned in the last chapter, is the first and most important step. It's the starting point. Understanding why, when, and how often you hit it is a different matter.

As I said, we all stop. Nonetheless, if we don't have an awareness at the core of why we've stopped and what caused it, we continue to repeat the same pattern. We've all done it, and it can become the most frustrating part of our lives when we're not receiving what we dream of, no matter how hard we work.

Coming up against your glass ceiling, the invisible barrier between you and your dreams, begins with a trigger. A trigger is an occurrence that precipitates a chain reaction which, if there is a lack of awareness of it, can become a horrible, endless, winding loop. A vicious circle and cycle, if you may.

A trigger can be internal or external. For most people the journey begins with something happening outside themselves. Someone says something, or something happens, and they react. This external reaction then triggers an internal stimulus, and depending on the nature of the stimulus, can become a sublime or vicious cycle.

A significant part of the world's population lives in this reactive state. We hear a lot about being proactive rather than reactive, but how often have you seen this truly happen, especially when it comes to us as individuals and human beings?

We can be proactive professionally in terms of thinking through, anticipating, and being creative in our work, utilising every part of us to get the job done, and done to the absolute best of our ability, and often we'll stop at nothing to demonstrate this.

What we don't very often see is people being proactive when it comes to responding to what may be triggering them in the first place, to end up in a situation they really don't want to be in.

As powerful as this can be in our professional lives, it has the power to change everything in our personal lives. This is why everything we're talking about; we will talk of at a holistic level. One change in our core at a personal level can alter everything professionally, and vice versa.

The reason for this is a lack of conscious awareness of the internal processes that occur and which we ultimately have control over, yet which many people don't believe in. They believe themselves to be the product of the world, of the external stimuli around them. They don't believe they have the power to be or do any other way other than how they've been told they ought to or believe they ought to.

"He made me say/do it."

"I can't believe she behaved that way."

"I can't help the way I feel."

We hear these words often, and they all imply we have little or no control over how we react to what is occurring, or if we do react, that there are certain ways of reacting. And often, because the trigger is subconscious and when it occurs we simply run on down that road without realising we are reacting to the trigger rather than the person or situation, the process remains subconscious. We never simply stopped and looked deeply into what just happened.

Being triggered is the key. It is the start of the descent down the rabbit hole.

So, what is a trigger? It's a spark, the thing that happened. The comment. The situation. For this explanation, we'll use an example of an external trigger and then move on to how internal triggers work.

It happened. Your manager made a comment, and you felt yourself react. Even if you didn't say or do anything, even if you felt you took a moment to pause and reflect. Often, we do it at a superficial level, in the sense of not saying or doing anything, but we still emotionally react to the comment.

What has happened is the universe opened a door through the comment your manager made, and in the moment of the comment you experienced an emotional reaction. You felt a particular way. An emotion or number of emotions stirred, bubbled, or erupted within you.

If the emotion(s) are strong enough, we will experience a fight or flight scenario, and we will react accordingly. If not, we may simply experience a sense of unease, discord, or be left feeling unsettled for the time being.

In this moment, how often do we stop and ask, "Hey, what is it *exactly* that I'm feeling?"

Naming the emotion is powerful, more powerful than you can imagine, because in the moment you paused, looked at it, and named it, you created awareness. Awareness begins the chain reaction. Naming the emotion allows you to take the next step in elevating your consciousness.

In experiencing the emotion, something drove the emotion. In the moment of the emotion, a thought was born, or recalled.

In this scenario, as per the first step of pausing and asking ourselves exactly how we're feeling and then naming the emotion, how often do we say, "Hmm. In experiencing this emotion, what was the thought I just had?"

Now this may seem like a relatively long-winded process. Let me say it's not. Once awareness is created (i.e., the trigger happens and you actively notice it and then go down this winding road), it can all happens within seconds. And when you become excellent at it, it can be instantaneous.

Usually that first thought leads to another, and then another, and so on. The thoughts coalesce, eventually round up into a belief or several beliefs you hold about yourself, others, your world, life, etc. By the time you've reached the beliefs stage, if you have never consciously gone through a process like this, the likelihood is you've decided as to what the original trigger or spark means to you and then acted based on it.

Understanding and knowing what triggers you—these can be positive or negative based on your perception—can open the door and help you see why you respond and behave the way you do, and how living this way has created your life and the experiences within it.

Wouldn't it be nice to *create* the moment rather than simply react, or respond to it?

This is very possible, and we will talk about this later in the book. However, before we get to that, for now, simply know that everything external to you is a potential trigger, and if you're not consciously seeing them, being aware of them and then making a conscious decision as to how to respond, you are living life on automatic pilot, creating outcomes that you may not want and might feel out of control.

Even if you don't feel out of control, you're someone who reflects deeply; ask yourself whether there are situations in your life where you've experienced the same unwanted outcomes. If so, then it means within your reflections, no doubt you have learned some truths, but the core issue remains elusive.

Internal triggers are far rarer, but they do exist. An internal trigger can occur through meditation or dreaming, and it too can release the chain reaction as mentioned above. The difference with an internal trigger is it's usually very subtle, and as with a nightmare or disturbing dream, it can impact you and you're not even sure why. You simply experience a level of being unsettled, and it can last for hours and days, only dissipating after it has left your memory.

Whether the trigger is internal or external, the way to work with it is to become conscious of it. Once we are conscious and aware, we have the power to change it. This is our power.

If you'd like to journal your journey using the *Six Steps to Six Figures Vision Book* and access the exercise pertaining to this chapter, please visit www.highvaluewoman.org/sstsfvisionbook and submit your details. You will be given immediate access. Enjoy!

CHAPTER 8

Getting to Know Your Glass Ceiling So You Can Break through It

In the last two chapters, we talked about what happens to you, what triggers you to hit your glass ceiling, and what processes you use to hit it. Understanding and having an awareness of these two things is something you can't undo. The next time you're triggered, I promise you, your mind will begin to start asking the questions you can ask of yourself by doing the exercises (you can find them here in the online vision book: www.highvaluewoman.org/sstsfvisionbook), and awareness is heightened incrementally each time you experience this process.

This is significant for a few reasons. One, your awareness of your emotions, thoughts, and what lies behind them no longer allows you to live a subconscious life. You'll find yourself reflecting far more on what you're doing based on where you end up, and you'll be able to trace back from what happened, the emotions you felt, the thoughts you had, and as you'll see when we get to step 3, the real reasons you behave and live the way you do.

Suffice it to say, the more you ask of yourself to have a conscious awareness of when you're hitting your glass ceiling (personally or professionally), the more you will take the time to pause, ask the questions, and find yourself waiting for the answers. Sometimes they will come quickly, other times they will be slower in arriving, and as you get better and better at this, you'll find the depth of your awareness increases. This means you're not simply receiving superficial awareness;

you're starting to delve into the marrow of who you are, and this is where the real treasure lies.

All journeys begin with a desire to change something that's not working, and change can only occur once we become aware, own what is occurring and then decide we are going to change it, and that we believe at some level we have the power to change it.

Knowing you have you very own version of a glass ceiling, one that may be holding you back, opens the door to the opportunity of looking at and studying this glass ceiling inside out, so you can begin creating strategies to break through. It also means you will now be far more aware of when another glass ceiling may be showing up in your life.

Life will always ask us to grow and evolve, and our glass ceilings can be a response to the fear we feel when we are asked to step outside our comfort zone. The transparency of the glass may mean we don't see the ceiling being built by the beliefs in our mind, but at least now we have a clear understanding and knowing of when we hit it, and how we can break it faster than ever before.

We've started the journey in this step of raising our awareness and consciousness of what we've been doing. In step 3, we will go deeper to understand the core issues holding us back, but to have the courage to do this work, we may need some deep and profound inspiration.

Step 2 is about the inner inspiration we may need to truly work through our obstacles, keep on the journey, and find what it is that makes it all worth experiencing and living.

Ready?

Step 2: Through the Glass Ceiling to Your "Why"

Uncovering why we hit our glass ceiling is a powerful step in and of itself, because it's only when the pain of what is, is no longer tenable that we begin to look for an out, a solution to what we believe is wrong in our lives or is stopping us from being and having what we want. When the pain becomes too much to bear, we seek relief.

However, relief for the purpose of relief is only a short-term solution, and in this book, we're not after short-term solutions. What I hope and pray you will choose for yourself are the visions and dreams you have for your life. Therefore, no doubt you're pondering why we're talking about visions and dreams when we've only begun to scratch the surface of what stops us in the first place.

Simple. We have only scratched the surface, and when we go deeper in step 3 to uncover what is really stopping you, there may come a time when you might decide, maybe this journey isn't worth it.

This is when a compelling, magnetising, out-of-this world dream or vision, and "why" is required. Why would you go through the challenges that will come before you, numerous circumstances where you will need to not only step out of your comfort zone but leap out of it, and the fear will be great, so what will help you make the leap?

You'll see a vision so bright, sparkling, and magnificent you won't even hesitate. A desire that brings tears to your eyes, goose bumps across your skin, and a delicate fluttering within your heart. A dream that simply has you saying yes with every part of you—body, mind, heart, and soul.

Care to join me?

CHAPTER 9

Who Did You Want to Be When You Grew Up?

When I was a little girl, I loved books. I still do, and whenever I think about or am asked how I loved to spend my time, now or as a little girl, I know a dreamy look comes across my face and I whisper, "Reading." There was and is nothing more intoxicating, enchanting, or mesmerising than a book, and to this day I am in heaven when I get the time to curl up anywhere and just read.

My passion for books led me to a deep desire for knowledge, and in my thirst for education and wisdom, I began to love sharing what I was learning. Often it was to an unwilling audience (made up of my younger sister and cousins from my very extended family, who didn't really have a choice), and we would play school, with yours truly being the teacher. We would spend hours playing this game, until eventually, they would slink off one by one, and I would turn around and see an empty room. I hadn't even noticed they'd gone, I would be so wrapped up in my teaching. Thankfully, I am a lot more aware now in my workshops!

I've also been called a geek throughout my career, as I would often be found with many books, articles, papers, journals—you name it, they were on my desk. It never mattered to me due to my passion for wanting to be an expert; I was happy to pore over them, knowing in my betterment, my manager, my team, my clients, and the organisation I worked for benefited. I was happy to wear my geekiness as a badge of honour, and I simply added it to my list of skills since I excelled at it and could talk about it with confidence and a certain amount of cheekiness at interviews.

When I finally incorporated my becoming a coach and writer into my twenty-year corporate career, my sister (who is also a coach, and who also loved to "teach" when she was younger) teased me, saying all those hours of playing teacher and being a bookworm had finally caught up with me. In that moment, I realised the truth of her words.

My childhood, and to an extent adulthood, passions have morphed into the work I now choose to do, and I remembered how this had always been my subconscious dream. I've always wanted to spend every minute I had reading, writing and teaching, helping people find the answers to the challenges they're experiencing from what I had experienced, learnt, and knew I had a skill and gift in.

The moment I uncovered my subconscious dream, a dream I didn't even really understand I had—it's always felt so natural, normal and a part of me—I knew that within all the seeds of the dreams and visions we have for our life and the people in it, our childhood can be the catalyst.

When we are under pressure or in stressful times, we find ourselves remembering a time when things seemed simpler. We loved life and couldn't imagine not doing the things we love. Then we grew up and were told we had to study subjects that would help us earn a living, and the death knell sounded for many of our dreams.

Some may have been lucky enough to have followed their passions, but for most of us this wasn't the case. We tucked our dreams and passions away and did our best to create a life where livelihoods and responsibilities drove what we did and who we chose to become.

This doesn't mean it must be this way and that what you're doing now, or how you're living your life, might not hold the kernels of your passions and dreams. I don't care what anyone says, it's never too late.

When I look back over my corporate career, I see the times that I've been the most successful are when I was learning new things, putting them into practice, making mistakes, solving problems, and teaching and coaching within my area of specialty and expertise. Of course,

I chose to be a specialist. I always aspired to being the "expert," the educator who shared my knowledge.

Even when I thought I wasn't living my passions and dreams, I was. Our passions die hard and often we think they've died, but in truth they haven't. They find ways of showing themselves in our lives, personal and professional, and simply because they aren't in the guise we know them to show up in doesn't mean they're not here.

Your childhood passions can be the key to what you love to do, and if you look very closely, I'm certain you can find within your life the many ways they are showing up for you. The key here is to become aware of them and consciously remember and imbibe into them the love, joy, and laughter that so often echoed when we lived them as children.

This one awareness, this simple reclaiming of who we really are and who we always wanted to be and do is the start of your journey to creating a true and ultimate vision and dream that will propel you to everything you choose.

At this stage, you might still be wondering how the above question ties in to what this book is about—which is helping you own yourself to such an extent you will never again truly doubt your magnificence—it will become clear to you as we move forward. I promise.

Owning yourself to the extent you can fully and without hesitation articulate the value you add, as a consequence of who you are, is something only you can do for yourself *because* of who you are, and every part of you is included in this. This includes the geeky girl who loved to read and teach (as in my case). Whether I was aware of it or not, it has served me deeply, as I am passionate about learning and sharing. In my career, I would do whatever it took for me to be and do this well.

Who do I want to be as a writer, teacher and corporate senior leader? Someone who inspires, delights, questions, and on occasions infuriates when I live 'outside the box'. I want to make you laugh and cry, get you to think, question, and be challenged. I want you to ruminate. I want to be kind, caring, and giving, a touch fierce at times, and most of all, someone you remember, want to know, and who makes a difference in your life—be it big, medium, or small.

This was who I want to be, because these were and are the people in my life—parents, family members, teachers, and friends—who did/do this for me.

I realise as a child I was very clear about what and who I wanted to be. It was only as an adult I became a little confused, but as my passions and dreams were always beckoning, I now see how I could be and do all of this and begin owning it in a way that was deeply authentic. It was me.

There are many people out there who do the work I do and may have the passions and dreams I have, but in the end, we all execute differently. It's this ability to know and articulate how you execute the things you excel and have a gift in, because they've been with you since childhood, that makes you stand out. Owning your gifts in your way allows you to talk about them from deep within you, and no one can take that away from you.

So, who did you want to be and why? What were the games you played, the costumes you wore, and the worlds you created? Why did you want to be that? What did you imagine you would do, become? Taking the time to find this out about yourself can help you understand and own why it is you are truly great at what you do, and who you become in the doing of it.

If you'd like to journal your journey using the *Six Steps to Six Figures Vision Book* and access the exercise pertaining to this chapter, please visit www.highvaluewoman.org/sstsfvisionbook and submit your details. You will be given immediate access. Enjoy!

CHAPTER 10

The Truth of You—from Your Childhood Dreams

As children, we live and die in our imaginations. We make up games, create the best homemade props, and don't hesitate to play our hearts and guts out. It's all very real, and I remember the loud moans that would resonate when one or more of the mums in the street where I grew up as a little girl in the north of England made it very clear it was time to come home for supper. We would lay down our sticks and stones and anything else we'd made use of and promise to be back the next day to pick up where we left off.

We didn't need anyone to tell us what the games would be; we made them up. We simply put on the mantle of who we chose to be and played the game, unconcerned with any outcome. It was pure, unadulterated fun.

Fast forward, and I still like jumping in puddles and swinging as high as I can go on the swings in the park, and it makes me smile when another playful adult joins me in the fun. Writing fiction novels allows me to let my imagination loose, and once again no one can tell me what I can and can't write. We listen to the voice within without stopping, and we hear what makes our heart sing and we do it. No holds barred.

This is because as children, we don't question the notion that we have dreams, and they can come true. We believed anything was possible and we played it. Sometimes, someone might be mean and say an idea of ours was stupid, but often we shrugged it off and played the game, or we went and played by ourselves. Nothing was impossible and we believed it, regardless of what anyone said.

Remembering who we were amidst our childhood passions and dreams may seem like a farfetched notion, and one that may not seem very useful as an adult, especially when we're doing our best to articulate how we add value and create the outcomes we do within our roles. However, as I mentioned in the previous chapter, the way we execute what we do from the space of our passion is different and unique, and to really feel who we are, sometimes we need to tap into the part of us that feels so "us" that we can simply and gracefully verbalise what it is that makes us utterly certain and immovable.

Wouldn't it be nice to feel such certainty and confidence? The sense of anything you think, say, and choose is yours and no one can deny it with any veracity? Yes, it's far more challenging as an adult with some topics, but when you're talking about *you* and how excellent *you are* at what you do that comes from a certainty deep within and you can back it up, who is likely to or can disagree with you?

Believing in your dreams and your ability to create them is a gift and skill as a child we never questioned. Unfortunately, as we grow up and are told to grow up (i.e., study subjects that will earn us a living), what we lose is our ability to believe both are possible. We simply filter the dreams out, yet we unabashedly go about creating our new reality. We create the success we want in our professional lives through sheer discipline and willpower, and there's something missing. Us. Our essence. Who we really are.

When we forget the heart-stirring and blood-pumping passion of what our dreams were and don't find a way to bring this into the work we do, we become passionless robots.

As I mentioned earlier, we all execute differently, but what makes the true leaders, the real movers and shakers of the world, stand out? They have a passion, a vision, and often a mission. They don't care that they may appear foolish. They demonstrate emotion in what they do and they make mistakes. They're willing to take a chance, big or small. They are the ones who move the followers into making them a leader and then they lead, and all the while we imagine there is something special about them, when in truth when we finally hear their stories, we hear of the dreams and visions they had as children that just wouldn't let them go.

Success in anything comes from understanding at a deep level there's nothing in your life that has happened that hasn't served you in some way, and the dreams and visions you had as a child were a significant part of that. Your dreams and visions were your own for a reason—so you could be the professional you chose to be, with the power of your dreams and visions coursing and pulsating within you, regardless of the career you chose.

How do you remember that part of you and bring it into your life, accessing a depth of dream and vision to make your skin tingle and heart sing? How do you find ways of slowly incorporating it into who you truly are in a way that makes you smile and the people around you glow, wondering what it is about you that has changed? Why would you make this decision, this choice of being carefree?

Simple. When you make this choice, and find ways of being and doing this, you inject life into you, your career, and your relationships, and the real you starts to shine through, creating joy for all concerned.

When I began accessing my true feminine energy in my professional life, it was as if a shroud had been removed from me. I've always been cheeky, mischievous and fun loving with a dry wit; however, I'd kept that part of me bound and gagged throughout my career, until I realised how little the people I spent over forty plus hours a week knew me. Even more so, I realised how much I wasn't enjoying my work, and wasn't bringing my best self to the table.

Within weeks, my team were wondering whether I'd met a new man, won the lottery, or was planning a big holiday. Joy leaked out of me. Horribly bad joke after joke, comments that had my team in stitches, remarks which dissipated tension in management meetings catapulted out of me, and I finally fell in love with my career, and it with me.

I thought I'd been successful before. Now, 'I' was being seen and experienced, and within the close confines of the corporate world, I received compliments that made my head spin. The productivity of the team soared. Work became a joy to come to and as tough as it got, I knew we would get through it because we, as a team had decided we were going to create the environment we wanted.

Owning this within myself gave my team permission to do this for themselves too, men *and* women, and we were all happier. This is not to say it's the panacea to all the world's ills—far from it. It was a tiny step to reclaiming who we all are, and how we could make a difference in the work we do, in the space we did it in.

Remembering and feeling deep within the things that made you burst with joy or simply simmer deliciously whilst you did them as a child is a sure-fire way of reconnecting with a part of yourself that has the power to transform the work you do and the success you can enjoy. Unleashing it is a gift to the world and a skill to add to your "success inventory."

So, what are you waiting for?

If you'd like to journal your journey using the *Six Steps to Six Figures Vision Book* and access the exercise pertaining to this chapter, please visit www.highvaluewoman.org/sstsfvisionbook and submit your details. You will be given immediate access. Enjoy!

CHAPTER 11

The Power of Intuition, and Your Inner Being as a Compass

Remembering the dreams and visions we had as children about who and what we wanted to be, getting in touch with the deeper traits within from that space delight and surprise us. We feel as if we could be anyone we choose, because we know it's who we are and who we're meant to be. This comes from a place we often lose touch with as we grow older—yet it's a place that holds the seat of our power, especially for women.

There is a space inside us that, when we take the time to stop, be still, and listen, we hear loud and clear. It's a voice designed to help us navigate the journey of life. As children, we didn't care what others said or thought. If we disagreed, this voice within would speak up, and in our childlike ferocity and passion we would often say things like, "But I just know!"

This was usually followed by a stern look from my father, and off to bed I would trot, steely in my determination that I was right. My dad and I still laugh about my stubbornness as a child, although now I tease him, saying, "It was always the pot calling the kettle black." We're very much alike. He disagrees, of course!

This voice is our inner compass. As women, it's a voice that, when we don't listen—often when things don't pan out the way we wanted them to—we may bemoan and make statements such as, "I knew it was a bad idea," or "I should have taken the other job," or "I knew I should have answered it the opposite way."

It's been called instinct, a gut feeling, sixth sense, or what works best for me, intuition. One definition of intuition is the ability to understand something instinctively, without the need for conscious reasoning. As children, we had many of those moments. We didn't question them and very often lived from them. As adults, we often ignore them, precisely because we can't consciously reason or rationalise them, and we know when we do make decisions based on intuition, the sensation is usually strong enough for us to consider it foolhardy not to follow through.

The downside, of course, to following our intuition is we can't articulate what it's really telling us, so we fall back to what feels like lame platitudes. "I can't describe it. I just knew." Many a good or bad decision is given either the accolade or blame when we make decisions using our intuition, and we're still left feeling as if something other than us directed what occurred.

Irrespective of whether you utilise this power within you, you know you have it, and it is a source of potential just waiting to be tapped into. As women, we don't utilise it, because we live in a masculine world where, if you can't rationally explain every aspect of your decision, there is scope for it to be negated or dismissed, and in the professional world, the very thought chills us to the bone.

Yet I know from my own career, often when I got a "hit" (my terminology for using my intuition), I would find ways of pulling it apart until I could pull it apart no longer, and I had sufficient information to be able to articulate it as well as I could to who I needed to. In turn, I could create powerful relationships with people when on occasion I would make enigmatic comments such as, "I just know it will work," or something to that effect. They would nod, and we'd be on our way.

Experience and expertise can help back up your intuitive hits to the extent people around you will trust you and let you do your thing, and from my own and others' experience, I know how compelling this can be. However, until you put yourself into the space of even allowing the intuition to come to you in the first place, you will never build this strength within you, and that is a tragedy.

Too many women recoil at the idea of living from a place of intuition, especially in their professional lives, yet it can be something that, once cultivated along with your unique dream and vision, can help you stand out in a way that radiates authentic confidence and certainty. You trust yourself completely.

How do we nurture this space, and what in God's name does this have to do with visions, dreams, and asking for what we want?

Simple. To have a magnificent vision and dream that is yours, because it's built on who you are and what you truly want based on what makes you, you. To begin with, we must tap into what your inner being is really saying to you in the first place. Your intuition or inner being is your inner guidance, and regardless of your beliefs, I believe it is the part of you that is connected to your higher self, the energy that creates world, God—whatever this is for you—and your intuition is the direct link to it.

It has been with you since before you were born, will be with you throughout your life, and will remain with you even after you're no longer here, present in this world. It is the combined wisdom of all that exists, and because of this, its essential nature, it will prompt, urge, inspire, pressure, prod, and on occasion shout louder than any voice you've ever heard, all to make sure you hear where it has the power to lead you back to your true self—your soul.

Your intuition is the vehicle for your soul, and your soul knows who you really are, why you're here, and what you came to do. It gave you many clues as you grew up—as a child, all the things you loved—to set you on your path for the rest of your life. What we've been talking about in these last few chapters is how this truth, *your* truth, has never been lost and is now about to be reclaimed in such a way that when you incorporate it back into your life as an active force, you will be amazed at the impact it will have.

From this space, everything you choose—how you speak, what you say, how you lead, work, live, and love—is embraced and embodied by your authentic self. All of it spills over in a way that no one else can ever emulate, and this is when you remember what I said earlier: you have no competition.

To begin living this way, of accessing your intuition, learning to hear and discern them to make sure you receive the real message, translating it into who you will be, converting it into action that serves everyone involved—requires first and foremost a decision that you choose to live this way. A half-hearted attempt is not sufficient, as your mind will try to rationalise what you're hearing, temper it into something less intense, and the ultimate outcome will be lost.

Once the decision is made, the fun starts. This is when we begin to truly play the game of life, and the key here is to play it like a game. This takes the intensity and pressure out of fearing you will hear something wrong, make a wrong decision, or say the wrong thing, and the way we do this is by starting small.

As with any game, we start by practicing with the smaller swings and kicks; we learn to tune in to our intuition by going back into our childhood and remembering how we used to hear this voice and act upon it. Then we can recall how well it worked for us and give us the impetus to start utilising it in other aspects of our life, once again starting small. We incorporate it into our professional lives until we feel it's now our friend, and the friendship is at the stage where you want it to deepen, so you begin asking more of it, in the sure-fire knowing your "friend" will not only rise the occasion but will elevate you far higher than you ever dreamed.

If you'd like to journal your journey using the *Six Steps to Six Figures Vision Book* and access the exercise pertaining to this chapter, please visit www.highvaluewoman.org/sstsfvisionbook and submit your details. You will be given immediate access. Enjoy!

CHAPTER 12

What Do You Really, Really, Really Choose?

We're now reaching the stage where you're probably noticing some changes occurring within you. Maybe your night time dreams are a little brighter, more lucid, and incorporating the things you really want in your life, and you're seeing how they could happen. Maybe you're noticing how much of the gorgeous, vivacious, smart, quiet, fun-loving, radiant, mischievous—whoever you were as a little one—is coming through more and more, or is already present in much of your life. You're simply seeing her influence more.

Whatever the changes, they are all perfect and a part of your journey. In the next chapter, I'm going to share a tool that will really help you empower yourself in every sense of the word. This will create something deep within you that will compel, attract, and pull you to making the ultimate leap for yourself—that of having the courage, confidence, and deep certainty within—to always be able to ask for what you want in your professional (and ultimately personal) life.

Before we get to that, I'd like to muse with you a bit more on vision and how to have a truly compelling vision that is what you want and choose. The reason I say this is that too often when we talk about what we want, it isn't what we desire deep within at a soul level—somehow or other, through everything we've lived, it's become what we believe we should want.

At the time of writing this book, I am forty-two years old and a relatively new entrepreneur. I left my very successful corporate HR career, made the leap of faith to become an entrepreneur and then decided to do both. I realise now, looking back at my career, my vision for it wasn't driven by my desire to be an expert in my field that would then enable me become an entrepreneur and really live my vision and mission: to be able to build schools for little girls in countries where they are denied education and therefore unable to be financially empowered and in control of all aspects of their lives.

In fact, this vision only came about because a dear friend made a comment a few years ago, that I should be teaching all I had learnt. I wanted to, due to my success, and I knew it could change many things.

As much as I'd had the dream of being an entrepreneur, after some failed attempts in my early years that are laughable now—I knew nothing—I'd resigned myself to a corporate career, never imagining I could do both. I aspired to the highest-level roles in my field, because I wanted to be seen as successful, having reached the upper echelons (not necessarily that I was).

This may sound bizarre, but ask yourself this. How often do we do the things we do because we have a genuine passion and desire for them, with no attachments to the outcome? Truly? For me, it's been and still is rare. I believe it's because we live in a culture where the attainment of success and the measures of success are utmost. It becomes for many about the destination—the outcomes, whatever they may be, and the journey, the process of growth, development, and evolution, fall by the wayside. It's a journey I'm still on and believe will be on for the rest of my life.

I also know some of you are going to be really confused. Right now you're saying, "Wait a minute, Sab. Aren't you writing a book about getting the very outcomes you're talking about?"

Yes I am, and as you go through this book, you'll come to realise what we've been saying from the start. It's not about the money, the promotion, or the raise. It's about who you become in the attainment of all of this, as you go about playing the only game in town—that of living the life you dream of.

Back to the point I was making. Often our visions, like many aspects of our lives, don't come from the essential and soul-connected part of us. Maybe yours does, but I know from many conversations that for a lot of us, they don't. They've come from and have been built up of many other parts—what we believe we should want, what society deems we should want, what our family and friends think about what we want, plus many others—to the point where, when I ask my clients to strip all of that out, to get in touch with what they really, really want (oh boy, now I'm quoting Spice Girls), they struggle.

It may be that when you take part in the utilisation of the tools in the next chapter, that what you vision and dream of is entirely your own. If so, congratulations, and I know it will simply seep you in deeper to this, and your soul will simply be further connected and inured to what you truly desire.

For those of you who aren't sure, let me share this with you. Connecting to what I call your powerful and priceless vision connects you not only to your intuition, it puts you directly in touch with your soul. Between the two, don't be surprised when you start being inundated with messages, coincidences, and occurrences that make you gasp.

Your professional life (your vocation and work) is an integral part of you, and the vision that can tie you into how you do this from now on will propel you to success you can't imagine. We're taking the brakes off. The exercises you've done so far have been preparing you, and once you start putting all of this together and most importantly, living your life from *all* of you, things will start happening that you can't even imagine.

Believe me, it happened for me, it's happening for my clients, and I know it will happen for you.

If you'd like to journal your journey using the *Six Steps to Six Figures Vision Book* and access the exercise pertaining to this chapter, please visit www.highvaluewoman.org/sstsfvisionbook and submit your details. You will be given immediate access. Enjoy!

CHAPTER 13

Your Powerful and Priceless Vision

From the hundreds of conversations with women I've had over the last twenty plus years about asking for what they want, one thing struck me more and more, and it became the heart of my business. I realised women wanted more than anything to feel powerful and priceless, because when you truly feel this way, you ask with dignity, and the conversation for the other becomes a pleasure too.

Nonetheless, when I ask women how often they feel powerful and priceless, they tell me it's rarely, and not at all when it comes to asking for what they want. When I dig deeper, I uncover that the idea of feeling powerful is often quite frightening, and the notion of feeling priceless is too far out of reach. Each time I hear this, and I still hear it too often, I am saddened.

Choosing to feel powerful and priceless is your innate birthright and something that doesn't need to be shouted out to the world, because by living it, everyone around you will simply experience it.

When I work with clients, I am struck with how often when we begin our work on creating their powerful and priceless vision, how much the vision is at a mind level. What do I mean by that? As a human being and soul, a vision can't simply be about goals in my career that then feed into my life. It took me a long time to understand and live this, especially as a woman. If I'm not enjoying the journey as much as the destination, the likelihood is I may be successful, but I won't be fulfilled.

When we begin talking about and building your powerful and priceless vision, it must encompass all of you, and therefore my version of visioning is called the powerful and priceless vision. This is about engaging all of you—body, mind, heart, and soul. That way, after you complete the meditation and visualisation (see link below) for this chapter, make sure when you build the physical version of your powerful and priceless vision, it covers the four points below. Otherwise you'll still be operating only at the level of mind, your intellect, and it won't be as juicy as you could make it!

Your powerful and priceless vision lives at four levels within you, and they are:

1. **Your Soul Vision.** This is the seat of all your desires and wisdom and is about what you really, really, really want and choose (which we discussed in chapter 12) at your deepest level. Sometimes this is the most challenging part of creating our vision, and we always start here.

2. **Your Heart Vision.** I call this "the real CEO of your life." At this level of vision, we take the soul's desires and wisdom and create a compelling and fulfilling basis for how to move forward and make it happen in a way where you will enjoy the journey *and* the destination. We will talk about this more in step 4.

3. **Your Mind Vision.** This is where we generally construct visions and turn them into goals. However, there is a difference with this way of visioning, which is why I like to call this level "the mindful COO." At this level we take the soul and heart vision—the compelling and fulfilling high-level way we want to be and live as we create this vision—and we mindfully create a plan of implementation, always being mindful of who we're choosing to be as we execute our plan.

4. **Your Body Vision.** At the final level, we have "the happy and willing servant"—our body, which will physically carry out the mind's plan. I use the word servant consciously. One of the true meanings of the word is "a person who is devoted or guided by something" (Merriam-Webster dictionary). I love this definition, as for me it is about serving and being of service, which is what the body does, as guided by the mind, heart, and soul.

Now we have all the components of our powerful and priceless vision, and the creation of it is a two-step process.

1. Listen to and immerse yourself in the meditation and visualisation that you can find in the online vision book, or if you prefer, you can simply access the audio recording from the website and use it in this way. Once you've read through it once, read it aloud and record it, and then begin by finding a space where you won't be disturbed for a little while. Burn some incense or candles, whatever you like, and take the time to really go deep. A shower, loose clothing, and some quiet moments for reflection and journaling are a good idea too.

2. Once you feel like you're hearing the truth about what you really choose in your life, and are beginning to feel the joy of having this as your vision, become like the child you once were, and physically create your very own powerful and priceless vision.

What do I mean? Build, paint, draw, collage, or sew it. Whatever creative medium you love, use it and create your very own powerful and priceless vision, and then put it somewhere that you can see it as much as possible.

My powerful and priceless vision consists of paintings. Some of my clients were like me and painted. Others drew or used pastels or watercolours. Some made vision boards, façades that contained all the inspiring visions they chose for their life. Some made clothes. Whatever juices you and fills you up, do it.

This is powerful, and as mentioned in the introduction to this step, it's a tool we need in our toolbox not only to inspire us and put in great place of power and passion as we make this journey, but more so for when it starts to get tough, and things aren't going our way, and we begin to forget why we started on this journey in the first place.

Connecting at all four levels in our vision will allow us to have options when things aren't going our way. Not in the mood to do? Simply connect with the feeling of it. Not connecting at the heart level?

Go back to the soul vision and tap into your deepest desire. Not there? Act, and you'll find the emotions will stir.

I've had many moments when all I've wanted to do is slip under the covers of my bed and stay there when it started to feel like it was becoming very tough to create what I wanted for my life. What I wasn't aware of is, as much as we don't want to hear it, sometimes everything might need to fall apart, because those constructs no longer serve us, and it's time to let them go. But we don't, and that's when the universe steps in.

The meditation and visualisation will help you connect as often as you need, to the truth of who you really are and what you choose to have your life be about. It's about becoming deeply conscious of what you want in your life, why you want it, and getting in touch with the power that creates worlds within you so you can start to create it for yourself. The physical creation of your powerful and priceless vision is to remind you that it's your creation, and you have the power to create it.

If you'd like to journal your journey using the *Six Steps to Six Figures Vision Book* and access the exercise and audio recording pertaining to this chapter, please visit www.highvaluewoman.org/sstsfvisionbook and submit your details. You will be given immediate access. Enjoy!

CHAPTER 14

Time to Play!

The last chapter was to help you understand that when we ultimately connect to why we believe we are here, everything, including our work, becomes part of this, and if you feel the work you're doing is not fulfilling, adding value, or making a difference, then I ask you to ponder on some thoughts below. We will talk in further detail about beliefs in step three, but for now I'd just like you to ponder with me.

If you believe you and your work are not tied together; it doesn't have a purpose, that your work isn't helping anyone, and it's not making a difference, what if you and everyone else in your field were to stop doing it? What would happen?

Now imagine that of everything within every industry. Even if you have political beliefs about business, corporations, globalisation, etc. for now, simply imagine if all work as we know it was to cease. What would happen?

In the beginning, as we make this journey, we may feel there is an incongruence between what your soul vision has shown you and what you're currently doing. This is fine.

The first time I had a soul vision of what my life and work was about, I couldn't figure out how being the head of reward for a large blue chip organisation was going to fulfil it. In fact, it seemed it was the opposite of what I was meant to be doing, which was helping educate and empower women at a soul level about who they really are, and building schools for little girls in countries where education for girls is either a no-no or considered nice to have.

It would only be four years later when a chance comment by a friend about a business idea, which took another four years to become a reality (my business, High Value Woman), that I understood how my entire career had prepared me beautifully now for my soul vision and work.

Teaching women how to ask for what they want so they can be empowered financially and ultimately in their life, and therefore don't have to face those dire statistics I mentioned in chapter 2, could only be done by me for me, after having spent over twenty years in a career that set me up for the business I now run.

Our career and profession is part of us and our lives, and for those of us who love our work, which I did when I was in my career but couldn't see how it would help me live my soul vision, sometimes it's simply a matter of trusting that if we love what we do, our soul vision is leading us, and it will unfold exactly when and how it needs to.

For those of you who love your work and it's already a part of your soul vision, then my intuition tells me you're reading this book because you want to experience receiving the money you want, gain the promotions you want, and have opportunities you want so you can be and do even more of the work you choose and have a life that is sustained by and supports it.

For those of you who feel a complete disconnect with your work and soul vision and don't feel you love the work you do, this is where you have the potential to decide. Why? Because the likelihood is you're doing the work you're doing because it funds the life you and your loved ones live, and you would like to receive more so you can have an even better life.

For all of us this is the journey of how your soul vision can translate into the work you do, which can become play, and you can get paid well for it. It happened for me; it happens for many women (and men) everywhere, and we simply must decide: Is this the game of work and life we want to play, or do we want to keep doing the same thing and getting the same result?

As always, it's your choice.

If you'd like to journal your journey using the *Six Steps to Six Figures Vision Book* and access the exercise pertaining to this chapter, please visit <u>www.highvaluewoman.org/sstsfvisionbook</u> and submit your details. You will be given immediate access. Enjoy!

Step 3: Drawing back the Curtains; Facing Your Truth

We live our lives based on a model of the world we believe in, shaped by the many forces that make us who we were, now are, and will become. These forces are often directing us at a subconscious level and only creep out into the light of day when we find that the things we truly desire in our lives appear to be eluding us, and we can't figure out why. Hence, our invisible barrier.

But as discussed so far, this is only the first step. Once we've remembered and rediscovered our visions and dreams and aligned ourselves to what is true for us, we must face the truth about why what we choose seems to still be out of our reach.

There is a space within all of us we sometimes dare not look too closely at, for fear it may show us how all that might frighten us is in some ways real, and to look upon it would bring it into being. Yet not looking at it is what keeps us frozen to the spot, controlled involuntarily by it, and our dreams and desires remain eternally out of reach.

It is time now to step up, take a deep breath, and with all that we are, draw back the curtain and with a strong body, powerful mind, loving heart, and eternal spirit, look deeply at what has held all that we choose for us, from us.

The time to unleash our courage is upon us. Come with me and let's brave the terrain together, and once and for all take back our power—the power to be and do all we choose, live the life we dream of, and ask for what we deserve.

CHAPTER 15

The Sum of All Fears

When I was a little girl I made the mistake of watching Stephen King's film *It* with my family. Clowns are supposed to be fun, and up to that point they had been. But no longer. After watching this film, the clown in the story became the source of my nightmares, which I must confess lasted until I became an adult. Whenever I had a nightmare, I would wake up drenched in sweat, trembling and terrified the clown was in my room, lurking in the darkness. He really became the monster under my bed, in my cupboard, behind the curtain. The most frightening aspect was the gut-wrenching terror I would feel in my nightmare, as I sensed his presence and always ran from it, not once daring to turn and face him.

As adults, we might still have nightmares, but the monsters morph as mine did, based on what frightens us, as we change. Having experienced nightmares and not understanding what they meant drove me as an adult to try to better understand my psyche and what was going on within. A rudimentary understanding of dreams helped me to finally comprehend they are the vehicle by which all that occurs inside us as our lives are being processed, and for me, this gave me the impetus to finally find my courage and face my "monster." I wanted to know who he really was, why he insisted on scaring the bejeezus out of me, and how I could rid myself of him once and for all.

I couldn't have known this would become the inspiration to the journey of my soul. At the time, it was simply a deep desire to know what scared me completely on those once-in-a-while occasions and make sense of it, so I wouldn't wake up petrified. I had heard about lucid dreaming and decided to give it a try. This is a powerful tool, and for anyone who has nightmares and wants to have the courage to face them—whilst in the dream—the results can be out of this world. I highly recommend it. It takes time, patience, and practice but is well worth the effort.

The first time I realised I was conscious in my nightmare was the moment I was rooted to the ground in absolute fear, sensing my monster behind me. I remember something inside me asking me to wake up, to take control of the situation as I had asked, and as I heard the voice within, my terror rose another notch.

But this time, so did my courage, and instead of behaving as I always did in my nightmare, which was to kick up my heels and run, I shifted my feet firmly into the ground and slowly turned.

My heart, along with every other organ, was in my mouth. Every instinct told me to run, that I didn't want to see what was behind me or could imagine what it had the power to do to me. It was this thought that changed my mind. For too long I'd allowed this fear to rule and paralyse me in my sleep and banish my sense of equanimity during the day. No more. It was time to face this monster and kick his ass.

When I turned and looked into the face of the monster, of course it got bigger and reached for me, and of course, I screamed and woke up. I was scared, but I was more annoyed that I'd given in. I determined once more to face the monster.

This went on for some months, and after a while I realised it was because I didn't have a clue what I would do once I did face it, therefore, my plan for encountering him changed. Instead of simply facing him, I would face him and ask him what he was and what the hell he wanted. No more Miss Nice Girl.

The next time I had the nightmare, the strength of my courage forced me forward, and I did turn and face him. But this time when he became bigger and reached for me, I put my hand out and simply said, "No. Not this time. This time, I see you."

The strangest thing happened. The monster paused, became bigger and roared at me, and once again, something that had triggered me the first time to stop, turn, and face it became stronger. As frightening as the monster was, it was no longer reaching for me, as if it no longer had the power to truly terrify me.

In that moment, I seized my opportunity and asked, "Who the hell are you?" and it simply replied, "I am everything that stands in the way of what you want."

This was when I became a tad peeved off, my fear beginning to diminish, as I stood in the wake of the monster of my child and adulthood, talking to it rather than cowering in front of it, and asked, "Why?"

"Because until you can face me, you can't face and overcome the things in your life that hold you back from what you want."

From then on, I began a dialogue with what I now know to be my representation of fear. Initially a scary clown from a film, then invisible demons, vampires. Whatever got into my psyche and had the power to terrify me, "it" used to make itself known.

We all have one. You may never have known, experienced, or seen it for yourself. However, just as the concept of fear exists, your personal version of it also exists, and it's made up of all the things that scare you, hold you back, and stop you from being, doing, and living the life you dream of. It doesn't have to be terrifying, but if it stops you, it has power over you.

Our fear represents many forces, and as we make this journey, the next step is to go deeper into why we hit our invisible barrier. This is where the truth lies, and it's when we must have the courage to draw back the curtain where all our fears lurk, and look in more detail and depth to what is going on. Why are we triggered by the things we're triggered by? Why do we have the emotions we do? What causes our thoughts? What is it that's driving us, and do we have the power to change it?

I believe these forces inside us, which we will delve deeply into through the next few chapters, become our model of the world, our core identity—our "operating system," if you will—and its power is such that if what you choose is not in alignment with it, it can never be. No matter how hard you try. Which is why we feel like we hit the invisible barrier time and time again and can never truly figure out why. We haven't got to the root cause. The core issue.

This is why we must go on the discovery of our inner selves through a process of conscious and holistic excavation, reflection, and meditation; so we can come to know who we really believe ourselves to be, and how it's impacting our whole life. Especially our ability to ask for and receive what we want and choose.

I wish I could say it would be easy, but you would be insulted if I did. It is simple though, yet there will be times when you think the things I'm asking of you are nonsense. You'll challenge me and be challenged by me. You'll put the book down and tell me to sod off, and for a while I will, and I'm fine with that.

Why?

Because I too behaved this way, as I made this journey, as have some of my clients. In the end, we all finally reach the point where we realise there's no going back, and the force that compelled us to begin this journey in the first place is now far stronger than our desire for safety or conformity.

As Albert Einstein once said, "A ship is always safe at shore—but that is not what ships are built for."

The same goes for us. We were never built for a life where we don't have and experience all that we desire. What we choose is a sign of who we are and what we want, a sign we must dare to follow and see through.

Part 1 of this book is about releasing our fears, but in order to release them, we must first understand them—know why they are part of our lives. As much as this statement will surprise you, I say it with utmost sincerity, and I know it to be completely true.

Our fears serve us. They are part of the journey, and they serve a purpose. They also, if not understood and known, become the darkness we run from and from which we never stop running. They take control of us, have power over us, and it is the strength of this power that subconsciously stops and sabotages us every step of the way. This is why it feels so damn hard to make our dreams come true!

Instead of our fears being part of the journey to help us grow, be, and do more, so we can live and give our truth and be rewarded in every way possible—instead, they drive us, and they are merciless. We know this from how horrible our nightmares can be, or the things that frighten us make us feel.

This is why in this step, together, hand in hand, we *will* draw back the curtains, face our monsters, and see them for who and what they are. In doing so, we release them to serve their true purpose for us.

Interested?

If you'd like to journal your journey using the *Six Steps to Six Figures Vision Book* and access the exercise pertaining to this chapter, please visit www.highvaluewoman.org/sstsfvisionbook and submit your details. You will be given immediate access. Enjoy!

CHAPTER 16

Drawing back the Curtains: The True Power of Our Beliefs

Making the decision to look our monsters in the face, the fears that may be holding us back, is an act of true courage and one that I commend you for. Not everyone is willing to make this journey, so the fact you're here and reading this—bravo! You're well on your way to releasing the little blighters and putting them in their place!

Earlier in step 1 I talked about how we are triggered, and once triggered we go on a journey, often one we're not even aware of in the moment. Something happens; we're triggered, we experience an emotion, and the emotion is preceded by a thought. That first thought leads to another and then another and so on. These thoughts coalesce into a belief or many beliefs you hold about yourself, others, your world, life, etc. and before you know it, you've given what happened a meaning based on all that, and from there you will behave in a particular way or take a particular action.

The lynchpin in this process, as you've no doubt garnered, is at the stage of beliefs. If you hold a particular belief about something, this will create a thought in line with it. The thought will then have an appropriate emotion attached to it; the emotion is what you experience, and from that place of emotion, often we act out a behaviour.

When we live this process subconsciously, we often feel like we have little or no control over what happens in our lives, and oftentimes we feel like we live the same situation in different guises over and over again. This is because the beliefs driving this process are the core engine, and until we know and understand what these are and how they are impacting us, we continue to live a life of reaction rather than creation, as beautifully articulated by Neale Donald Walsch in his *Conversations with God* books.

At this stage, this is the model I outlined in step 1, categorised into the various phases:

1. Something happens, and you're triggered (i.e. you experience certain emotions).
2. Your emotions are powered by thoughts about what just happened.
3. Your thoughts are driven from beliefs about what you believe just happened.
4. You create meanings to what just happened based on the beliefs you hold.
5. You behave in a particular way based on what you believe what just happened actually means.
6. You behave in a certain way, and your behaviour creates certain outcomes and results that then have an impact on your life.
7. The cycle continues.

At this stage, we've only talked about the first three phases. We're now going to look more deeply at the engine of beliefs that is driving what thoughts you're having and creating the emotions you're experiencing.

Beliefs can be created by what we have lived previously, and what we have lived previously can create the beliefs we hold. They can become references for what we believe to be true, because we've lived them. It's very hard to disagree with people's beliefs when they've lived them, and it's very true for them. Their experience tells them it is so. Beliefs can also be what we take on from other people, for example, from our family, community, culture, and society.

If we have empowering beliefs about the things that happen in our lives, we feel empowered; we act empowered; we feel like our lives move forward, and it all serves us. The converse is also true. If at any level you feel disempowered or out of control, and all the new-age stuff about how we create our own reality seems utterly farfetched, this will be also your experience because you believe it to be so.

A belief process has the power to be a sublime or vicious cycle, depending on how much you believe the above to be true for you. If you've never experienced this for yourself, please feel free to test the hypothesis in reference to your own beliefs. I know once I became aware of this, I played with it endlessly and it simply became a new way to be. My consciousness rose exponentially once I started to see how this could be and was true for me.

To get to the core issues, we must make this journey first, the journey of beliefs, and this part is critical. Without it we're unable to go deeper and uncover the root issues that may be keeping all that you don't want firmly in place, subconsciously sabotaging your every effort.

Beliefs really run the engine of our thoughts. It's where our thoughts originate when we have a perception that could be based on what we've experienced in our own lives, or simply been told what is, and in the absence of evidence to the contrary, we believed it. In believing it, we act out a behaviour in line with the belief and therefore continue to perpetuate the experience.

Changing our beliefs can change our lives, but beliefs can be very ingrained, and if we have beliefs that we have taken on from others, changing them can mean a change to our core identity—who we believe ourselves to be—and this is often the biggest stumbling block for many when it comes to looking closely at what we truly believe. Changing a belief can potentially mean a lack of connection, a loss of friendship, relationship, or family unity, and due to this, many would rather step back and continue as before. The perception of the gain isn't worth the pain of the perceived loss.

Sometimes it's not as intense, and the change is a positive one for all concerned. Saying that, it's only fair as you make this journey and begin delving into the depths of your beliefs that you understand what you're undertaking. I know being on this journey for me has been challenging, but it's also been rewarding, and although the times of challenge were tough, I knew the change required of me was what I wanted at a soul level, so it happened.

Working with beliefs is a powerful process, and one that can change your life. Be gentle with yourself as you begin asking yourself the questions that will lead you to the answers you seek.

If you haven't utilised the vision book yet, you might want to start at this point as there are some great exercises that will truly add value to what you're learning here. You can find it at the following here. www.highvaluewoman.org/sstsfvisionbook Submit your details and you will be given immediate access. Enjoy!

CHAPTER 17

Uncovering the Truth about Our Monsters—the Beliefs of Fear

To help you truly understand the part your beliefs play in this process, we're going to break them down even more and pick them apart in a way that will help you see them for what they really are.

I am a firm believer that everything in life is energy, and the science of quantum physics has been bearing this metaphysical concept out with the many discoveries it has been making in the last fifty to sixty years. I'm not a physicist by any means (I failed physics in high school); nonetheless, from my limited understanding, I have come to comprehend the premise that everything, at its core, is energy. The more you break matter down to find its core, the more you uncover that within the space there is something buzzing in there. It's not solid, and it's not empty.

The most fascinating thing I've read about quantum physics is the notion that things don't exist in isolation in and of themselves, and when we observe matter, it changes. Our very attention to it makes it change its behaviour. The first time I read this, somehow it made sense to me, and it began my educational journey to get my head around quantum physics even more, and what the teachers of the ages have been saying for so long. When you focus on something, it changes or behaves differently.

Why is this important?

As we continue to delve into beliefs and how they impact our lives, driving our thoughts, emotions, and behaviours, resulting in the outcomes that are created, we can potentially start to build a picture of how what we believe in is creating the world in which we live.

As I said before, you don't have to take my word for it—try it out yourself and see what happens.

Right now, though, I'd like to continue breaking down the different types of beliefs we have and how, when we hit our invisible barrier, it might feel. It could almost be said to be hitting a metaphysical energy block.

The language I will use here is based on the coaching methodology I utilise in my practice, and if you're interested in learning more, please visit http://www.ipeccoaching.com. You can also get a copy of the excellent book associated with this transformative methodology, *Energy Leadership*, written by the creator and founder of the IPEC (Institute for Professional Excellence in Coaching) school and methodology, Bruce D. Schneider.

Energy Blocks

When we hit a barrier, we effectively hit an energy block, meaning the energy that has the power to move us forward has been blocked. Most energy blocks exist due to beliefs that do not serve us and hold us back from being who we truly are and creating what we truly choose. They become blocks to our journey to awareness. If something is not blocking you, then your whole process of beliefs, thoughts, and emotions is serving you and you are flowing—even more so, your awareness is usually high.

There are two types of energy blocks, outer and inner. This is similar to triggers, where we had external and internal types. We will look at them both, but what we are interested in most of all are the inner blocks, as they have the most impact on us and are within our locus of control.

Outer Blocks

An outer (or external) block is that thing outside of us that is perhaps outside our control. How we feel about and deal with an outer block determines how we live and function in our lives. If the outer block has the power to stop us in our tracks, or we use it to stop us, then we are allowing it to have power over us. If we don't find ways to overcome, work with, or simply remove the outer block, it can significantly impact us and our lives.

Generally, when people feel at the mercy of things that are happening to them, they can feel victimised, and they tend to struggle moving forward. Working with outer blocks usually involves tools, such as reframing, or looking at the beliefs we hold about the power of those blocks.

Inner Blocks

Inner blocks are those produced within us and if we're honest, generate most of the barriers and blocks we perceive to have in our lives. Inner blocks disrupt and distract us, and they can derail our attempts to create and accomplish what we choose to have in our lives. Inner blocks can have tremendous power over us because they are inside us, and if we are living or operating with any level of unconsciousness within our lives, the inner blocks simply magnify in power until we either allow ourselves to believe all that is happening to us is because of things outside our control (outer blocks) or we hit the ultimate barrier and we decide, "No more."

Inner blocks can be broken down into four main categories:

1. limiting beliefs;
2. assumptions;
3. interpretations; and
4. "monsters"

Limiting Beliefs

Limiting beliefs hold us back from success. If we don't believe something is possible, we won't even try at it, and even if we did, it wouldn't be as strong as it could be, because at our core we don't believe it. Often, we accept a limiting belief as true because we've learned it from someone else, from something that happened to us, or from some other authority such as the media, a book, or a movie.

Limiting beliefs are general beliefs about the world, our environment and situation, and the people around us that stand in our way. Changing limiting beliefs can be done several ways. These include providing evidence to the contrary, exploring the effects the belief has had on our lives, looking for proof or lack thereof for its truth, or simply modifying the beliefs or aspects of the belief so they serve us better. Not every belief needs to be discarded. Sometimes it just needs to be changed.

Assumptions

An assumption is believing that because something happened in the past, it is going to happen again. Assumptions are more personal than limiting beliefs and more intimately involve us and those around us.

Assumptions are debilitating because statements such as, "I know it won't work because I've tried it before and it didn't work," are prevalent and stop us in our tracks. Even if we were to try, it won't be as strong, as if we really believed in it.

Challenging an assumptive belief is simple. We simply ask the question, "Just because it happened in the past, why must it happen again?" One of my favourite teachers, motivational speaker Anthony Robbins, taught me early on in my personal development journey the principle that "the past does not equal the future." It's one that has stopped me from making false assumptions on many an occasion!

Interpretations

An interpretation is where we create an opinion about an event, situation, or experience in life that may or may not be true. Many people believe their interpretation of anything is correct when in fact it's only their viewpoint. The truth is there could be many viewpoints about the one thing being discussed.

Interpretations are like assumptions and can be directly challenged by asking, "What's another way of looking at that?" Looking at situations and other people's opinions and seeking out other perspectives is also a very good way of challenging our interpretation about something.

"Monsters"

Our final inner block is the most powerful of all. It has many names: inner critic, judge, gremlin, demon, or monster.

Our monster is the voice within us that tells us not to try, never to take a risk, always take the safe road, and to compromise the happiness in our lives by playing it small. The message from our monster is that we're simply not good enough to reach the summit of success and gain what we want—our dreams.

All inner roads ultimately lead to the monster and "I'm not enough"—whatever "enough" may be. Monsters are highly personal, rooted deep within us, and carry the most intense emotional charge of any of the blocks mentioned above.

Working with the monster energy is what we will be doing in the next few chapters, but it's useful to know what all the blocks look like, because once we have an awareness and knowledge of them, when we come across a belief that isn't serving us and we want to delve deeper into what it is, at least we now have the tools to do so.

Visit www.highvaluewoman.org/sstsfvisionbook and submit your details. You will be given immediate access to a visionbook full of exercises to help you on your journey. Enjoy!

CHAPTER 18

Your Monster—Your best friend?

The blocks that arise from the beliefs we hold and that have the power to stop us in our tracks, either for a moment or for the rest of our lives, ultimately all have their core power in one statement. Throughout my corporate career and as a coach, I have come to know and understand that beneath all the things holding us back, the ultimate sponsoring thought and belief is, "I'm not enough" or "I'm not worthy."

This isn't a challenge only for women; it's a challenge many men face too. However, given this is a book written for women, I will aim my discourse at this audience.

If you've taken the opportunity to work with the beliefs process from chapter 17 through the utilisation of the vision book (see link below), you'll remember I talk about "sponsoring thoughts and beliefs." These are the core thoughts and beliefs from which all your thoughts and beliefs spring. When you do this process and get to this point with something that has been stopping you, you'll know in your gut, "This is the one," and I can guarantee every single one is a shade of the ultimate core belief I mentioned above of "I'm not enough" or "I'm not worthy."

This is what is classed as the monster energy in the methodology I utilise as part of my coaching process. The monster is the voice I talked about in the introduction that lets you know any time you're thinking of trying something new that you don't have what it takes, you'll never succeed, you're kidding yourself, and that really, you should sit down, be quiet, and do as you're told.

I'm certain we've all heard that voice and the words, which can vary in vocabulary, degree, and intensity. When we've allowed this voice to be our truth, it does stop us in our tracks, and we come up with all the reasons why what we want and desire cannot happen. Its arsenal begins with the blocks we talked about in the last chapter, and before you know it, we've sat down, shut up about what we want, and reverted to who we were before we dared to dream.

Monster energy is highly personal. This is because our version of "I'm not enough" or "I'm not worthy" usually stems from our past.

As a child, we dared to dream, imagine, and play. For a while this may have worked well for us, and if we were lucky enough to have parents who allowed us to be, we may have thrived and blossomed. Then we went to school, and suddenly we had to behave in a particular way. Our physical freedom was curbed, and slowly our mental and emotional faculties took a beating too. When we didn't conform, we may have been penalised or punished, and as we grew older, more and more influences began to determine whether our behaviour was appropriate, and before we knew it, we began to censor, manage, and alter our behaviour to make sure we fit in.

One of my most favourite quotes is from John F. Kennedy, who said, "Conformity is the jailer of freedom and the enemy of growth."

My childhood was very much about conformity. I was born into an Indian Muslim culture and conformity was an absolute given, and as many people in my family and around me will tell you, it seems I wasn't born with a subservient bone in my body, which meant conformity was a hard gig for me. My poor parents! We laugh about it now—we sure didn't at the time!

I struggled with conforming, simply due to the fact I was deeply curious and imaginative and liked asking questions when things didn't seem to make sense. In a culture where asking questions was frowned upon, I was blessed to have parents who would do their very best to answer them, and well, if that failed, I always had the library. In the end my journey and the journey my parents took with me was a challenge, but I can say I have no regrets—not sure if my parents would say the same!

The process by which who we were naturally as children evolves and amends is a complicated and complex process, and I'm not an expert in this area. I think we can all agree that still, as we grew older, we did make decisions based on what happened to us and how people responded to us when we were younger.

As humans, we crave connections and when we don't receive them, especially unconditionally, we will do whatever it takes to get them. Some of us learn later in our lives this is the pattern we've been running. Some learn earlier, yet others never experience such a realisation—or if they do, they become deeply regretful, to the point where they struggle to now live their lives. They are so caught up in what they did or didn't do in their past, something they cannot change. For some, this is a tragedy they never recover from.

From the start of the process when we are triggered, this is the journey we take, usually back to things that may have happened in our childhood that are so painful we bury them deep inside, and the wall of protection is built. We change who we naturally are to make sure we never experience such pain again, and this is the space where beliefs can be formed that impact our whole lives.

The opposite can also be true in the case of positive experiences. We have an experience; we drown in positive emotion, and our bodies grab everything happening within us. Before we know it, we have a reference that supports the meaning we have given to what just occurred.

As we're talking about being blocked and stopped to the extent we can't move forward, we'll continue our deep dive into the beliefs that hold us back. Something happened that we perceived to be deeply painful, and from there, we gave it a meaning. From this space a belief was created, and it's a subconscious process that was stored deep within. It became something we lived without ever really knowing it, and the more we lived it, the more we reinforced the belief, and the truer it became for us. This is what I mean when I say it's very hard to argue with people's beliefs if they are living them.

Monster energy epitomises this space, a space of pain that has the power to debilitate and in the ultimate sense "end" us. People who have fears that run their lives—phobias, for example—live in this space, and it is an awful space to be in, as subconsciously we equate it to death.

Now you can see why bringing awareness to this can be such a frightening process and journey. You're being asked to look deeply at what it is that scares you. Even in this process the monster will rear up to try to terrify you into stepping away.

Courage is what's required in dealing with monster energy, and you're not alone as you take this journey. Before we get to that, we must delve a little further into the composition of monster energy.

It's the voice we hear often, especially when we step outside our comfort zone. When we hear it, our natural inclination is to stop in our tracks. This is how most of us behave, because firstly, the voice is subconscious; we're not even aware this is what it is, so when we keep hitting our invisible barrier, often we don't even realise this is what's happening. We either stop, and that's the end of the line, or if we're motivated and inspired enough, we will move forward. However, when it comes to the things that really matter to us, it's usually the former until you've explored the whole of the latter premise.

Therefore, if we're stopping, pausing, or simply not moving forward because we're subconsciously listening to this voice that is telling us quite vociferously how bad our lives will be—how terrible things might become or, to an extreme, how we could die if we don't listen to it—we can imagine the emotions we would experience in this space. Yuck! Enough to make you go running and screaming (metaphorically speaking, of course) in the opposite direction, and in that moment, your monster energy has won. It has stopped you from growing. But is that really true?

I'd like you to consider this. In the moment you experience your fear—you don't say what you wanted to say, didn't take the action you desired—did the monster really stop you, or was it simply trying to protect you from experiencing all the awful things it imagines will happen if you moved forward with what you think you want?

This is a powerful moment of awareness, and I'd like you to sit with it a while, and then when you've reflected on it for a bit, if you like, have a go at the process aligned to this chapter in the vision book and see what comes up for you.

If you'd like to journal your journey using the *Six Steps to Six Figures Vision Book* and access the exercise pertaining to this chapter, please visit www.highvaluewoman.org/sstsfvisionbook and submit your details. You will be given immediate access. Enjoy!

CHAPTER 19

Who's the Big Bad Monster? Taking Back Your Power

As we begin to ruminate on who and what the monster energy really might be in our lives and how it impacts us, one thing we can't dismiss is the real fear we can feel when we face something that scares us. Whether it's bungee jumping, leaving your job because it's no longer right for you, walking away from a relationship, asking your manager for a promotion and raise—whatever it might be—the fear in the moment is very real and has the ultimate power to stop us in our tracks and halt the movement of our lives onward and upward.

Fear in one aspect of our lives can spill over to the other parts, and the damage can be extensive. People will stay in destructive personal and professional relationships due to fear, and as discussed before, the reason for this is we believe at some level we can't make the change. We believe we don't have what it takes. We're saying we're not enough.

In the moment of our abject fear, when we are facing what frightens us the most, many women tell me they picture the fiercest, scariest thing they can imagine, and in the moment of meeting it, they freeze.

I talked to you earlier about the face of my fear for quite a long time—Stephen King's clown in *It*. Damn clown! I'm not frightened of it anymore (I don't think), yet it still has the power to make me shiver. When the clown morphed into my next level of fear, I continued using the tools of meditation and lucid dreaming to help me confront it.

Both tools helped—meditation at a conscious level, lucid dreaming at a subconscious level.

But what was frustrating me the most was the fact my fear was continuing to morph. I still hadn't truly uncovered what the ultimate message of my fear was. It just kept changing its guise. Through all my reading I firmly believed fear was serving me, yet I couldn't figure out how. My fear of fear wasn't diminishing, and I knew it was because I hadn't experienced its truth.

I became like Indiana Jones on a quest. I knew my fear had a message, and would always have a message throughout my life—I simply had to figure out what it was. Each time something came up that frightened me, I would whip out a piece of paper or my journal and ask myself question after question in my attempt to pick to pieces the core of my fear.

As you can imagine, it was exhausting, and I was no nearer to solving my mystery. At this stage my fear had morphed into an invisible demon, so I couldn't even see the damn thing. In my dreams it terrified me, and in my waking moments it was horribly nebulous, which meant any time I felt it was even in the vicinity, it would move away and scare me in a different manner.

Your fear won't let you get close, because the closer you get, the deeper you look, and the likelier it is you will see it for what it is.

Finally, one night I had a breakthrough. Hallelujah! I was having a nightmare. I was in the house I had grown up in, in one of the bedrooms upstairs where I knew my younger sister was sleeping, and I had felt my invisible demon's presence. I was utterly petrified and crying, yet I climbed the stairs, determined to keep my little sister safe. In the darkness of the upstairs hallway I waited with my breath caught in my throat until I knew it was around me. I wanted to run away, I really did, but the thought of my sister kept me there, and the thought that if I didn't face it, I would be forever running. I decided this wasn't an option. I wasn't going to run anymore.

I sensed it behind me, closing in, and once again I made the decision to confront it. I turned and felt it, and I spoke, my voice full of fury, which surprised me. "Show yourself to me."

The demon laughed, which really didn't help, but I stayed my ground. After a while it began to take a shape, and what showed up was the last thing I could ever have imagined. Can you imagine it?

It was *me*. My fear had morphed into something I couldn't see, something I battled with on a regular basis, as I tried to understand why the dreams I wanted so badly weren't happening, and all along, the thing I had been battling … was me.

Now, at this stage some of you will no doubt be thinking, *What? What is she talking about?*

That's okay. I'll finish the story and hopefully it will make sense.

Our fear is cunning and will do whatever it takes to keep you frightened, frozen, and stuck. The minute you make the decision you're going to face your fear; your fear will do whatever it takes to make sure you never do.

Demons were always a horrible fear for me. Like the clown, it stemmed from my childhood—once again from watching a Stephen King movie, *Salem's Lot* (you think I'd learn!)—and this one took me into my mid-thirties to face it, so it was a biggie.

All my life I'd lived *my* ultimate fear version of "I'm not enough" as "I'm not enough to be loved." I've been single for most of my life, therefore my life bore this out, and it was this, that had prompted me on this journey in the first place. In my obsessed drive to prove I was lovable and worthy, I became very successful in my career to prove my worthiness (I had no idea at the time this was what I was doing), and the thing I feared the most was that the belief I had about myself would be true, that regardless of everything I *did*, I was utterly unlovable.

So I kept myself very, very busy—creating career success after success, constantly stepping out of my comfort zone, moving countries, writing and publishing novels—whatever it took, I did it. That way, I'd never have to stop and face the truth. That maybe I was unlovable, and that I'd never be loved, no matter what I did.

This is the reason my invisible demon was utterly terrifying and turned out to be me. I was running from myself and my inability to face my biggest fear.

This was a pivotal moment. In understanding my fear was my

86

un-lovableness, my perception of deep unworthiness, having to turn and face it—the fear I had been dreading facing for so long—and then experiencing the truth of what I had been running from made me realise a lesson that changed my life.

In facing myself and the belief I had about the supposed truth of myself, I had to look at myself completely, warts and all, and I came to a startling realisation. When you stop and face the very thing that frightens you the most, the simple act of facing the fear gives you the power to know. The fear no longer has power over you.

In looking deeply at what I had been running from for so long—me—I completely forgot to be afraid. Once again, I had a dialogue with myself to understand what was going on.

What I learned was this. Fear has two functions: one, to keep me safe from the things I perceive to be unsafe and which may cause me pain and, as discussed above, these usually stem from experiences, in which we experienced deep pain. By making me frightened of them, I may take the time to reconsider, or I may move forward in the hope I dissipate the fear. Either way, I feel the fear and either do it—as Susan Jeffers so beautifully taught us to be and do, in her best-selling book, "Feel The Fear & Do It Anyway"—or I don't. Both of which have consequences, and I drop the fear or I increase it.

Secondly, if I face the first function of fear and dissipate it, fear gives me the opportunity to be more than I ever dreamed of being. FEAR is, as one of my favourite teachers, Neale Donald Walsch, said, "False evidence appearing real."

FEAR is asking me to look at it, know it's not real, and move forward, to become more than I ever dreamed. When we live like this, and we all have, how alive do we feel?

This is the ultimate gift of fear—to show us the things we're afraid of, whatever they may be, and however they may have come about. In the end they're not real, and it's only by looking deeply at them that we can see the truth.

When I finally faced "me," I had to encounter all the things I'd lived and done in my life, mostly great, some not so great, but all of which had served me and brought me to where I now was. In that moment I knew, I liked, and I loved who I was, realising everything had played a part, and I didn't have a single regret. I could look back over all of it, see it for what it was, and own it deep within me. And in that moment, I loved "me" unconditionally.

This is when I knew I could own all my successes and failures, and I could articulate them with profound authenticity because they were mine, and no matter what, I loved me. In this state, I also started truly seeing and experiencing how loved I really was, which I never allowed myself to experience previously.

This was an enormous gift. In facing my biggest fear, I found my biggest love: me.

Ready to meet yours?

If you'd like to journal your journey using the *Six Steps to Six Figures Vision Book* and access the exercise pertaining to this chapter, please visit www.highvaluewoman.org/sstsfvisionbook and submit your details. You will be given immediate access. Enjoy!

CHAPTER 20

Who Do You Believe You Really, Really Are?

To believe "I'm not enough" or "I'm not worthy" at any level requires us to have the core identity of someone or something that could possibly ever be "not enough" or "unworthy." In the journey of discovery we are undertaking, we are peeling back all the notions we have about ourselves, from what triggers us all the way to what, how, when, and why. In this process, we're delving deeper and deeper to find out where all of this originated from, and this is where we land—at who we ultimately believe ourselves to be.

This may be a very reflective chapter for you. It will ask you to look at some of your deeply held beliefs, which is exactly what my intention is. As chapter 17 demonstrated, what we believe in all aspects of our lives drives what we think, feel, and do, and in the end, it creates our lives from all of that. Our belief about who we truly believe ourselves to be creates all of that.

How? I hear you ask. By being the powerhouse that drives the engine and operating system of our beliefs about everything in our lives and beyond.

If our belief is that we are simply human beings—physical beings with everything that entails—and at the end of our lives we will be gone, and then, based on what this means to us, we will operate from this core belief. Now, this core belief may be empowering or disempowering—we decide this depending on how we live our lives, the choices and decisions we make, and the results these create—but in the end this model drives everything.

If our belief is that we are human beings having a spiritual experience—a physical and non-physical entity with the ability to tap into everything that exists—again, based on what this means to us, our operating model made up of beliefs about everything will drive our thoughts, emotions, behaviours, and actions, creating results and outcomes aligned to this overriding notion.

Both models work because we make them work through our attention, focus, and action. As discussed previously, how hard is it to disagree with someone's belief when he or she is living it? It's nigh on impossible, because that person believes it, lives it, and the power of his or her belief and the following through creates exactly what is believed.

Belief often feels like it exists at a cellular level. Often when we believe something, we'll use words such as, "I don't know why it feels like that, I just know it's the truth." Belief ultimately leads to knowing, and in knowing we can be resolute, even if we can't rationally explain why. We just know.

I believe personally from my own life and experiences that life is a self-fulfilling prophecy due to our level of belief and knowing, and in the words of another of my favourite teachers (God rest his soul), Dr. Wayne Dyer, "You'll see it when you believe it."

This is why *who* you believe yourself to be is utterly powerful, and why it can completely stop you in your tracks or exponentially move you forward. If your belief about who you are is in any way contradictory to who and what you choose to be, do, or have in your life, because this is a belief that goes to the heart of you—*it's who you are*—then your very core will not allow it to happen, because it will not make itself wrong.

Think about it. Have you ever experienced a time in your life when someone was proved wrong, but because of his or her beliefs at the core level, the person still disagreed with you?

This is the power of your core belief about who you are, and who you believe yourself to be, and how it can end at a deeply subconscious level any dream you have that contradicts who it believes itself to be. It also has the power to infiltrate all subsequent beliefs you may ever hold about yourself, others, life, the universe, etc. It will not allow you to be out of alignment with itself, and this is where it becomes critical to truly pull back the curtain, as in the famous scene in *The Wizard of Oz*, and understand who is pulling the strings.

One clear, deep look at the sponsoring beliefs you hold about yourself and who you are has the power to unravel and release every belief you ever held about yourself and your life that doesn't serve you. You can now see the truth, and it's not who you believe yourself to be anymore.

When I finally became brave enough to look at the biggest fear I had about myself, which had permeated every aspect of my life—that I was unlovable—I saw all the beliefs I had created, and which I lived, as if my life depended on it, because to an extent it felt like it did. This is the dread of your ultimate fear that somehow it will equate to death of some kind, and to avoid and run from death—i.e., not being loved—I did everything in my power to be successful in the hope someone would see my outer success and find me worthy of being loved.

When I finally laid this ultimate fear and the core belief of me within it to rest, as much as I had been incredibly successful, my success had an underlying sense of emptiness. As if I hadn't been myself, I hadn't truly enjoyed and loved what I was doing, and no matter what I did, it would never be enough. I had to keep chasing the external professional success that would allow me to feel worthy in the sweet hope that in the end I would be loved.

Letting go of this fear entirely changed my life. I unreservedly changed my mind about who I believed I was, and from here, all my beliefs changed. I knew, believed, thought, and felt loved in and of myself, and from here it didn't matter if I was single or not, if I was successful or not. What I had wanted all along was this intense, deep knowing of my true nature—that I am Love and loved—and from here, the outpouring of it swept through every part of my life.

I loved myself, loved others in my life, and I began to love my work. I cared less and less what others thought of me. I would happily listen to their opinions, but I no longer needed their validation, and I didn't feel the need to agree with everyone anymore. I spoke from a place of deep certainty, confidence, and truth about who I was, what I could do, how I had already demonstrated a lot of it, how I could be even better if they gave me a chance, and I trusted that if something didn't pan out for me it was because something better was waiting.

The focus of my life shifted from a space of lack—something was missing in me that I subconsciously had believed made me unlovable simply because I was single, when all around me, I was surrounded by people who loved me—to a realization that there was nothing missing in me, never had been, never would be.

The change in me at my core changed everything, and when you do this work to create the success, opportunities, and financial rewards in your professional life, don't be surprised when aspects of the rest of your life change too. This is the power of your core belief about who you truly are, and it will change everything.

If you'd like to journal your journey using the *Six Steps to Six Figures Vision Book* and access the exercise pertaining to this chapter, please visit www.highvaluewoman.org/sstsfvisionbook and submit your details. You will be given immediate access. Enjoy!

CHAPTER 21

Money, the Biggest Monster of All

We've talked a lot about beliefs and fear and how together they can halt your journey forward in insidious ways we don't consciously realise. It's only when we start pulling apart the whole construct that we realise just how enmeshed we are in a structure that may or may not serve us throughout our lives.

As we near the end of step 3, one topic is deeply intertwined with beliefs and fear, and due to the fact it's such a huge topic, I'd like to bring it into your awareness and consciousness so you can begin to understand the impact it has on you. At the end of the day this topic is the subject of why you're here, so let's get to it.

Your beliefs about money—what it is, who you are in relation to it, and how you interact with it in your life—all show up when you imagine having the conversation about what you want to receive. The minute you make the decision you want to receive more—the thought of asking for the money and to an extent, justifying why you should receive the money—all merge, and again, at a subconscious level, take you into the space of your beliefs about who you are and what money is to you.

For a long time, I had (and still do) many beliefs about money that I had never consciously considered, other than on a fleeting, superficial level. I had done work with some amazing teachers including Tony Robbins, and as invaluable as these experiences were, they still hadn't taken me to a space where money became a natural outflow of who I was choosing to be and what I was choosing to do. I was still stumped.

My biggest limiting belief about money was, "I have to work really hard to earn good money," and boy, was I working hard! My parents had always instilled a strong work ethic in me, but I had reached a point where my hard work wasn't serving me anymore. In fact, I was simply exhausted. I felt very much like a hamster on a treadmill, and the idea I could be truly wealthy seemed farfetched, even though I was receiving excellent six figures. I'd reached a point where the idea of receiving higher six figures seemed impossible—there weren't enough hours in the day to work harder than I already was!

What annoyed me more was how, in our society, we keep hearing about how it's possible to be wealthy and do what you love, and there were many examples, yet for me the puzzle was incomplete and I was bone tired. I didn't want to do any more. I wanted to find a way of doing the work I loved and be paid well for it.

It was only after I experienced my breakthrough around my core identity that I really started questioning all the beliefs I had about money as part of the overhaul of all the beliefs that had sprung from my previous fear and core identity. The minute my core identity changed—I now recognised and remembered myself as pure energy and a part of all that exists, which meant nothing was, is, and ever will be separate from me—this changed how I saw money.

I went from believing I had to work hard for money—because it was something outside of me that came to me because of the effort I put into it—to believing that if I was pure energy and a part of all that exists, then money wasn't something outside me. It *was* me, and my ability to experience it came down to one thing and one thing only: who I truly believed myself to *be*.

This was a challenge in and of itself because it required me to get even clearer about who I was, why I was here, what my purpose and vocation were, and how, in the end, I would live and give my gift. It was only when I owned who I was at my core—the good, the bad, and the downright ugly—that I could articulate the value *I* added in my own powerful, charismatic, and compelling way. I stopped competing with others because I knew that even if someone had the skills and experience

I had, that person couldn't be me and couldn't bring to the table what I could, and I learned all over again what it was to be and live me.

There were times when I didn't get the job I went for, but the jobs, money, and opportunities I received were really the ones that were right for me, and soon I entirely trusted this process. It didn't lead me anywhere except to here and now, which for me is my dream.

I learned money is energy, and when I live and give my gift fully with all of me, no apologies, it's as if the universe celebrates big time and brings more my way. I don't work as hard anymore, now my work has become my purpose and vocation in the truest sense of the word. It's how I would choose to spend eternity. I'm not the kind of person who would ever retire, and now I have work that fulfils me in every way, and I know, although it will change, as everything in life always does, at least now I've found my space, and I am being rewarded for it very, very well.

Our relationship with money can be complex, deep, and at times utterly irrational and frustrating. We can feel like we're banging our heads against many brick walls when what we want isn't coming our way. Ironically, as it always seems to be in life, the more we want it, the more elusive it seems to appear.

A key aspect of being able to ask for what you want is understanding that as much as you may think the coming and going of money in your life reflects the value you add, if you haven't made peace with your relationship of self-worth to money, you will forever live the cycle of feeling the tension of asking for money and disliking or even hating the conversation. You may feel outwardly confident, but if there is any resistance within you when it comes to asking for what you want, it will leak out of you, and the person on the other side of the table will subconsciously sense and react to it.

I'd like to share something with you. It's what I talked about earlier, and it bears repeating. Through my own personal experience, what I know for sure is this. No one can ever pay me what I am worth because as a human being, a soul, I am priceless. What they can pay me for, however, is the significant value I add, financial or otherwise, when I authentically and powerfully live and give my gift.

Decide who you are, what money means to you, and please know this. Asking for what you deserve is not arrogant. It's knowing your worth inside out, being able to demonstrate and ask for it, so you can continue to give your gift even more. I can't imagine a stronger reason for anyone to ask for what he or she wants. Can you?

PART TWO

~Own Your Worth~

'It's not what you call me, but what I answer to.'

~African proverb~

Step 4: Uncovering the High Value Woman Within

Once you've faced your fear and truly understood why all that was holding you back no longer has any power over you—because you are the power of you—now the time is rife for uncovering the jewel, the diamond hiding in the dark, the preciousness of you. This is crucial in being able to ask for the money, promotion, or opportunity you want. It comes from a deeply authentic well of truth, the profound truth of you deep inside.

Within you are the keys to the kingdom, your kingdom, and you get to choose what it looks like. You already have a vision of it. You've lived your truth and your worth in moments throughout your life, and in those flashes, you've felt your power, radiance, divinity, and uniqueness. Deep down you know there's no one like you, but you dare not like yourself too much in case someone might deem you self-absorbed, self-centred, or God forbid, selfish.

No longer. It's time for the voices outside you that have tried to tell you for so long who you are, how you should be, and what you should do to quiet down, and your true voice, the one that has been whittled down to a whisper, needs to be heard.

It's time to let the shadows loosen and drop for good, the muck covering the jewel to fall away, and the whisper scrambling in the dark to step toward the light and become a wondrous song. The time is here; the time is now.

'I AM Woman. Hear Me Roar!'
—Helen Reddy

CHAPTER 22

Getting Crystal Clear on Your Powerful and Priceless Vision

We're now entering a space that is all about remembering. This is because who you are at your core never went away. She simply hid for a while, or for some of us, for a very long time. When we get further into this work and you start seeing glimpses of her and then more, the sweet sensation of finally recognising her as our truth can bring tears to your eyes.

This is because you've come home, the space where the truth of you resides, and now as you work to uncover and own her again fully and completely, you will discover the ultimate truth.

Your true power always comes from within you, and you are connected to a power that creates worlds, therefore you don't need to truly seek anything outside of yourself. Ever.

When I say you don't need to seek anything outside of yourself, I don't mean in the logical, factual sense of seeking knowledge, for example. What I mean is you don't need to look for the answers pertaining to yourself at your deepest self, outside of you, as any answer about you will always be found within. This is learning to hear the voice of your true self; your intuition and trusting it will never steer you wrong. It's a journey and it takes time, and the rewards you will reap when you reach the point where you don't need external validation as part of your life will seem like the sweetest reward you could ever receive. This is when you will begin to laugh loudly, live freely, and love unconditionally, and your light will dazzle those watching you. I can't wait!

To get cracking in this chapter, we will focus on practical strategies and tools that will allow us to uncover the powerful, worthy woman we know ourselves to be, and through step 5, how to live her every day of our lives so we rarely experience a moment of doubt or questioning. This is the ultimate aim.

One of the most powerful tools we have at our disposal is, as mentioned previously, our imagination. Napoleon Hill, author of *Think and Grow Rich,* said, "Whatever the mind can conceive and believe, it can achieve."

If at any point in your life you haven't been able to do this, and believe me I had the same problem, what I learned was that it wasn't through a lack of will or trying. It was more likely a lack of alignment of what I truly believed and what I was trying to create. If we don't believe in our core with every fibre of our being, we will not create what we are aiming to create.

Therefore, we will focus on the next two steps, as to how we take the power we now have, because we have faced our fears and intend to turn it into the fiery flame of passion, purpose, and progress. Then by the time we get to step 6, where action reigns supreme, you won't doubt you can do the things I will recommend you do to receive what you desire and choose for your career and life.

Owning our worth is integral to doing what we came to do. It's owning the power we need to overcome any obstacle, stay the course, and ultimately reach a point where we can love everything that comes our way, no matter what. We start to see it for what it truly is, an opportunity to be and grow into more than we ever dream of.

The way to begin this step is to reach back to step 2 and remember the "powerful and priceless vision" you created for yourself. This is what you choose, and for you to create this, we're now going to chisel away at the dirt covering the diamond we are and see for ourselves the gorgeously bright jewel we now want the world to experience.

To do this, I would recommend carrying out the powerful and priceless vision meditation a few times, so you can really feel what it feels like to be this woman, living this life. The more you practice this meditation and see your vision in what you have created as you work through these exercises, you will notice that you really are uncovering "you," and to an extent you are recreating her to live more and more fully in every aspect of life.

Once you have carried out the meditation several times and feel as if you could quite easily articulate the woman in the meditation you imagine being, give yourself a name or a label that resonates with you and defines this woman you know you are and now will begin to live.

To help you, I will share with you my definition of who I knew I was and was beginning to uncover. She became my High Value Woman and incidentally became the name for my new business. Below is my definition of the woman I now know myself to be and am forever aiming to live each day. You can use High Value Woman as well. Many of my clients do!

I Am a High Value Woman

A High Value Woman knows her worth and understands her value in and to the world around her. She is clear about who she is and who she chooses to be in each moment, and she lives this with intention and integrity. She holds herself responsible for all she creates, owns her successes and failures, and has an ardent desire and passion for learning and growth in every part of her life. She is courageous in her heart, following it first, in conjunction with her mind, allowing love in the truest sense to be her guide. She recognises and acknowledges her power as a strong, feminine woman, appreciating that no one will ever truly fathom who she is, because only she will experience the truth of her being from the depths of her body, mind, heart, and soul.

A High Value Woman is a woman of her own, living from the inside out—passionately perceptive, playfully powerful, and purely priceless.

If you'd like to journal your journey using the *Six Steps to Six Figures Vision Book* and access the exercise pertaining to this chapter, please visit www.highvaluewoman.org/sstsfvisionbook and submit your details. You will be given immediate access. Enjoy!

CHAPTER 23

The Power of You— Owning Your Worth

When I first began working with the definition I had created of myself as a High Value Woman, she was fashioned first and foremost out of a powerful remembering I had from carrying out the powerful and priceless vision meditation daily, each night before I went to bed.

The night I finally wrote my definition of her, she was crystallised into the core of me, and knowing she was me and I now intended to live her in my day-to-day life, I knew she would change the way I saw myself in every way. I also knew that more than anything, she would change how I would live her in my professional life, especially when it came to having the courage to ask for what I really wanted.

I'd never truly struggled in asking for what I wanted. I'd found a way each time, but there was always a sneaky niggle inside me that somehow, they would figure out what an impostor I was. I know now this is a common fear for both men and women, but from my experience and conversations with many women, this goes to the root and core of them, so no matter what they say or do, the niggle never goes away. Once I knew and felt who I truly was deep inside, it changed me indelibly, and I knew I would rarely question my worth again. I may have doubts, but never again would it have to do with my sense of worthiness.

The concept born within me that night, and which integrated itself into me completely, was the understanding that no one is ever going to be able to put a pound or dollar value on *who I am*, because I am inherently priceless as a human being and soul. I can, however, find a way of articulating and allocating a pound or dollar value on the significant value *I* create in the work I do through who I am, all that I bring to the table, and it is this which will help me and many women like me *ask* for the money, promotions and opportunities we want. And I know they are ours to have and own.

Through this process, I believe we will create more female leaders, own our true place in society and begin to change the world, so women everywhere can have the kinds of opportunities we all deserve.

The minute I got this was the minute my real desire for my business High Value Woman and the mission aligned within it was born. When I learned to embody and live "her," with the twenty plus years of experience in the international reward and remuneration industry, the two created a magical alignment, and my true mission was born. I had lived for this moment, and the second they had fused into the deep knowing of what my passion and purpose were, I knew I would never again shy away from being able to ask for what I wanted.

I didn't, and I haven't. Even in my business, when I first started out and I had the entrepreneur's nightmare of figuring out what I should be charging because I knew I had lived this throughout my life, sometimes subconsciously embodying what I knew at a deep level, I knew I could ask for what I wanted, through my ability to demonstrate the significant value I would add and continue adding.

This is the power of owning your worth and learning how to articulate your value. The two go hand in hand. One gives you the solid, profound, unquestionable certainty of who you are; the other, learning how to articulate what you do that creates the outcomes your managers and organisations need (much more on that in step 6) and allows you to ask to share in the rewards created from your efforts.

This is why chapter 20, "Who Do You *Believe* You Really, Really Are?" is critical. Your sense of worth comes from your ultimate beliefs about who you are, and the more your beliefs strengthen the notions you hold about being a priceless human being and soul, the more you will live this and be the beacon of a leader who sees this in others, and encourages them to be and live this too. Another sublime, upward-progressing cycle!

It is never simply about us. When we step into this place of authentic voice and power, without realising it we not only give ourselves the permission to shine, we give everyone else the opportunity too. This is why when women get together and work in real sisterhood, we do change the world. We are far better at collaborating than competing, and as we all live and give our gifts, we come to the truism I mentioned earlier: you have no competition because no one can be you.

So how do you take the vision of the woman you dream to be—the vision you hold within yourself that is now becoming real for you each time you meditate—and connect to her in a way you can begin to live her in all your life, especially professionally?

This is the task of the exercise associated with this chapter, which you can access through the link below. Here you will take the vision of what you're seeing and imagining and begin putting the flesh on her bones. This is the remembering of her in a way that resonates with you and only you. By doing this exercise for yourself, you reach down into your depths and pull out what calls to only you.

This is not to say when you do the exercise below that other women won't come up with similar attributes as you. What it means is she is yours and always will be, as she came from you, and the attributes you choose will be demonstrated by you in your own inimitable way. You brushed off all the dirt covering her and slowly started seeing her shine.

In the next few chapters we will talk about the crux of the change for any woman making this journey—the power of feminine energy—a subject that creates heartache and pain for many women, as we imbibe the barbs of society that deigns to tell us what it means to be a powerful, feminine woman. We don't need anyone to tell us what it means to be her, but after thousands of years of stamping down and trying to obliterate the feminine and often divine feminine power, it's not easy to embrace this lost part of us in a way that requires very little outside interference. In fact, it's the only way we truly can. That and find ways of reconnecting to other women who are making the journey too.

Please do use the online vision book exercise (<u>www.highvaluewoman.
org/sstsfvisionbook</u>) that will allow you to create a heart map of who you truly believe yourself to be. We are going to unwrap, uncover, and reveal the diamond that has been hiding deep within.

Are you ready?

CHAPTER 24

What Do You Stand for and Believe In?

To know who we are, to be this person and live intuitively and instantaneously, we must know what drives the attributes and characteristics we chose earlier to embody as part of the woman we dream of and intend to be. From all the work we've done earlier regarding our beliefs, we now have a view of who we intend to be, so what does she stand for?

In our day-to-day lives, we are asked to make decisions about who we choose to be, and we can only do this when we know what it is we stand for, based on our beliefs, and then demonstrate this by living them in every moment. This builds character, and this is how we experience the world and the world experiences us. When the two align, we are congruent, powerful, compelling, and unstoppable. When they don't align, we cease to be true to ourselves; the world experiences us as such, we feel powerless, and that insidious energy of "not-enoughness" pervades everything we do.

In every aspect of our lives, we must know who we are, what we stand for, and how we will show this to the world. It helps us set boundaries and non-negotiables—behaviours we will or won't tolerate—and helps us articulate these to set expectations for the people around us from the beginning. When we live this way, as much as conflict is a part of the world, it doesn't need to be a daily battleground for us and the people in our lives. We set expectations early on. It's when we don't live what we say that conflict is created, and disunity sets in due to the confusion that abounds when we say one thing and do another.

Values can change as we have experiences. I know I'm not the woman I was two years ago, never mind the woman I was twenty years ago. Life has shared many of its treasures with me, and as I live, grow, and evolve, this is my constant, something I know people around me might struggle with, as it can create uncertainty.

Throughout my journey of growth, this is something I am very aware of, and I seek to share it when it is right for me with the people in my life. We must never be afraid to communicate with and show the world through love who we are as we grow. If we're afraid we will be loved less *because* we have grown and changed, then the bigger tragedy is the love we bear for ourselves—our sense of self and worth—will diminish faster than any love outside of us. We and the world will be experienced as far less than we are due to this. No matter how many times we hear that change is the only constant in the world—we must find a way of embodying it in every aspect of our lives.

So, what do you stand for? This is a big question and can go into many layers and depths, but for the sake of clarity in this book, I'm going to keep it as simple as I can.

I'd like us to think about values as guiding principles we choose for our lives, based on our beliefs and how we wish to live this life. Values work can be intense and satisfying in that once we have clarity about what is important to us and why, we can then live this in every way for ourselves and most importantly communicate it to everyone else. That way, people know who we are.

This isn't to say we dropkick all our values on people the minute we meet them! Not at all. This would be like turning ourselves inside out on a first date, which would not only be completely off-putting but would take the gorgeous mystery out of who we are!

Knowing, understanding, and living our values is about having this clarity for ourselves and then in our lives, letting them be seen, heard, and known in whatever appropriate medium is required.

One of the biggest mistakes people make when it comes to values work is to have so many values that we not only are unable to prioritise them, we can't live them authentically. It was Alexander Hamilton (a Founding Father of America and chief staff aide to George Washington) who said, "Those who stand for nothing fall for everything."

We don't want to be this kind of woman. When we struggle to know what we stand for, we come across as yes-people in every sense of the word, and people struggle to get a feel for us.

We want to uncover the values that are inherently important to us, because they feed who we are, who we choose to be, and how we choose to live in the world. They are also a demonstration of the vision and mission we came to live, so when you get to the exercise for this chapter (link below), make sure you do the exercise thoroughly and reflectively, as an integral part of the journey of uncovering the magnificent you that you are.

Values have power. They define us in every moment and show the world who we are. Instances in our lives can change our values, so hold on to them until they don't serve you anymore because you have grown and evolved. Otherwise, what are you holding on to?

The best way to know if your values are still what you stand for and believe in is by having them in front of you, or showing up in a way in your life where you know instantaneously what is true for you. Organisations have their values often everywhere to remind employees of how to act. Our lives require no less, and every six months or so ask yourself, "Is this who I am and who I choose to be?"

Changing your values can be as challenging as understanding and knowing them in the first place, especially if others are concerned. Therefore, it's important to be able to talk about them with the people in your life in a way that supports all of you. As we've discussed, change is frightening, so if this is a process you choose to live, how can you involve the people who matter to you?

The more awareness and knowledge people have about you and who you are, and if they have an understanding that you're going to change, the more comfortable they can get when this happens. This may take time. One of the biggest complaints you hear in relationships is, "You've changed," often said in an accusatory tone. The person who has changed shrinks, feels bad, and ultimately imagines he or she has carried out the biggest betrayal.

The truth is, the biggest betrayal of anyone is to assume you won't change. It is an inherent part of life and nature that we must evolve or we die. Maybe not in the physical sense, but how often have relationships, jobs, and friendships died because someone refused to change?

Everyone has a right to decide how their lives will be and what they will stand for. If you're someone who loves growth and evolution as part of life, share this message with love. Let them know. Take them on the journey too.

If you'd like to journal your journey using the *Six Steps to Six Figures Vision Book* and access the exercise pertaining to this chapter, please visit www.highvaluewoman.org/sstsfvisionbook and submit your details. You will be given immediate access. Enjoy!

CHAPTER 25

Tapping into and Living Your True Power—Your Feminine Energy

We're now heading into the heart of this work. This space for some may initially be a bit uncomfortable; for others, the feeling will be of coming home. In the end, we all find the space right for us to occupy as we move forward.

One of the biggest challenges women experience is living in a very patriarchal, masculine world. I also mentioned previously that it's what I call a "false-masculine" world because it's not a representation or reflection of the true masculine quality either. It's a way of being in the world that has been around for a very long time and where true feminine energy is no longer seen, represented, or revered in the ways it used to be. It's not valued as a powerful way of being.

From the research I have been doing in understanding how as humanity we have come to be where we are, there is a model of the world that anthropologists and archaeologists have been discovering. It existed thousands and thousands of years ago, and doesn't rely on a "dominator model," as defined by Riane Eisler in her excellent book *The Chalice and the Blade.* Neither gender dominated. This was a partnership model, where the sexes utilised and lived their true, inherent natures with the intention of collaborating with each other for the good of all, rather than competing for the benefit of the few.

The reason I make mention many times the notion of who you believe yourself to be at your core is for the simple reason it was leading you all into the space we are now going to journey into together. It may be a journey of joy, delight, happiness, and love, or it may be a journey of pain, despair, sadness, and heartache.

Why? When we don't live truthfully in and from our core, it's as if someone took our very soul away, and our ability to live fulfilling lives in all aspects of our lives is severely diminished. Therefore, it is a journey we must make if we wish to live as our authentic selves.

Later in this chapter I will share with you a way to know whether your authentic self is feminine or masculine at her core, but before I get to that, I'd simply like to muse with you on my journey through this precarious and often confronting time as I sought to reclaim my feminine power and be the woman I knew I was but was not living.

As I've shared with you, I grew up in a very traditional and patriarchal culture, and as progressive as my parents were, it didn't remove me from the rest of the cultural influences around me. Attending my religious school, I drove my teachers mad with questions they didn't want me asking. As a teenager, I gobbled up books to prove women were not in any way inferior to men, so I could tell this to the boys and men who argued with me that we were. In the end, I was determined to be a success in this world and prove them wrong.

To say I was driven would be an understatement. I began my working life doing part-time work when I was thirteen years old to create the feeling of financial independence, and the minute I received my first pay packet, I knew I never had to be dependent on anyone, especially not a man. All I'd ever heard from my culture was how my role in life was to find a husband and become a dutiful wife. I completed university, working all the while, and began my HR career knowing I would succeed at everything I touched.

By the time I was thirty I had already become the head of a function for a subsidiary for a significant international company, and I was exhausted. I loved my work, but my doing the work felt like it was slowly killing me on all levels. My personal life was non-existent. Vestiges of my culture made it tough to be a woman in the Western world, creating a clash of values that in the end served me to decide who I wanted to be.

It was only when I reached my mid-thirties, still plugging away, still being successful that it was finally revealed why, underneath all the success, the core of me wasn't feeling successful. It is a journey many women experience, reaching pinnacle after pinnacle of success, yet often feeling the emptiness once reached, only to ask, "Is this it?"

I desperately wanted to know why the work I was doing, the work I loved and excelled in, wasn't fulfilling me the way I knew it could. It was only when I finally discovered that I had been creating all my success within the framework of a strong, masculine paradigm that I had found the answer.

I was pretending to be someone I wasn't. This also ties in to what I want to share with you about who you are at your core—feminine or masculine—and how this one answer has the potential to change everything for you.

We live in and out our lives, men and women, in a false-masculine form in a false-masculine world. Even men often struggle with feeling successful and fulfilled in this paradigm, because it isn't catering to their true, masculine core either. Therefore, imagine if, at your core, who you are and how you want to live is the opposite of what you're being and doing most of the time. How would you feel?

To me, it used to feel like living someone else's life or living in someone else's skin. I created success after success in my professional life by living false-masculine principles in everything and in the process negated who I really was. She was a powerful, feminine woman who ended up in a very small, dark space, where she waited until I rediscovered her and remembered who I really was.

When we remember the true nature and source of our power, we are unstoppable. We can see in our world today what is happening when there is an imbalance in the natural course of life. For thousands of years the model of success has been the dominant false-masculine model of success. This model is also embedded in the power structures of our society, where the feminine is being subconsciously and systematically denied, and every generation has continued to perpetuate the model. This is where we now are.

The challenge I feel is in truth; no one is succeeding or being fulfilled in this model, except for a few, and even then, I question whether they are truly fulfilled. There is an inherent imbalance in this model, and I believe in the balance of life and nature, and when one way of being plunders another, we all lose.

Suffice it to say, in the collective model of the world, where women have had to fight for the right to the vote, along with many other basic rights denied to us for so long, we did so in the model of the world we've been living in. This is to an extent still the world we live in, although it is changing, but the fact remains. Our lives and patterns of success have been created and governed in a powerful false-masculine world, and we have tried to create our professional success on a very un-level playing field, playing the game by rules that weren't created by us or for us.

Therefore, what happens when a powerful feminine woman constantly lives a powerful false-masculine life? For some this may work, and later you'll see why. For most it will wear them down and out, and they'll forget who they are. Even worse they will continue to perpetuate the story we keep telling ourselves about how this is the only way it is, and if we want to be successful, this is how we will do it.

I know I did, until I learned it could be different. I learned through one of my favourite teachers, Tony Robbins, the model and concepts of masculine and feminine energy. In the beginning, almost fifteen years ago, I learned it intellectually, but that was it. It was only when I finally understood the true implications of the work that my life changed dramatically, and I also found out who the person behind all of this was, David Deida. David writes more from a relationship perspective, and if anyone is interested in learning more about this topic, please check out his website, http://www.deida.info.

I have paraphrased the main aspects of his concepts of feminine and masculine energy for this book and my coaching, so I hope he'll forgive me if I've made any undue assumptions.

David talks about how we all have a core energy that gives us the power to embody who we really are as men and women—feminine or masculine—in all aspects of our lives. (To be clear, the terms masculine and feminine for this explanation are not gender- or role-based; they are descriptors regarding our core energy or essence, and I will shortly discuss this more later).

When I talk about core energy or essence, it is in the sense of who we are at our centre, a way of being that naturally fills us up and allows us to be whom we are, and live and give our gifts naturally.

Feminine and masculine energies are required to live a full life, but when we consistently and constantly live in an energy that isn't our core, it leaves us drained, exhausted, and unfulfilled to the point where we question why we're even here.

According to David, approximately 90-plus percent of men are masculine at their core, and 90-plus percent of women are feminine at their core. A man and woman can either be feminine or masculine in their core—as stated before, this is not about gender—and the best way David suggests to discover your inherent core is to answer this question: "In a romantic situation, do you want to be ravished or be the ravisher?"

If you want to be ravished, you are feminine in your core.

If you want to be the ravisher, you are masculine in your core.

The exercise can seem a bit simplistic and it may be, but it works, and to gain a deeper understanding of the essentials of feminine and masculine energy, below are my paraphrased version of the definitions that I've taken from David's book *Intimate Communion*. This is a fantastic book that I would highly recommend if you'd like to explore this topic even deeper.

Masculine Energy or Essence

Masculine energy is directional, single-minded, always involved in a mission or project, and sees life from a transcendental position: it likes to stand above and outside of things such as emotions, thoughts, and knowledge so it can see and experience them from a detached viewpoint.

From this perspective, everything is fixed in life, concrete, and therefore, can be perceived as a limitation or trap. Masculine energy seeks to be free, is always seeking freedom, which is why commitments can be seen or experienced as having to leave "the transcendental realm of endless possibility and enter the earthbound realm of endless responsibility" (David Deida, *Intimate Communion*).

Masculine energy is directed to the sky, the energy of god, the desire to fling off any kind of shackle and experience itself as a strong, directed power in the universe, cutting through any obstacles in its way and achieving its ultimate aim. Masculine energy is all about *doing*.

Feminine Energy or Essence

Feminine energy, on the other hand, is all-flowing radiance in every direction. It seeks emotional fulfilment, wants to be filled up, can stir itself up into a snarling lioness or purr like the teeniest kitten. It is the energy of the goddess and can be wild and unpredictable, or nurturing and life-giving. Its primary modality is emotion and feeling, the ability to know and experience the depth of human emotion, to live it in complete fullness in tune with life and all that entails.

Feminine energy is at peace in life, in sensuality, in the natural elements. It's grounded in the earth and flows with the force of life. It knows instinctively and inherently what is required from any situation, especially where people are concerned, because it knows life and the sensitivities of life. It is intuitive, open, and unstoppable and attracts everything to it because of its inherent connection to life.

Feminine energy epitomises relationship—it wants to relate to all of life and is all about *being* and feeling.

When I first read the words describing the two types of energies, as much as I adored the definition of feminine energy, I knew I didn't live it. Often, I ensured I stayed in my head rather than my heart, so I could cut through everything to accomplish what I needed and wasn't surprised then in my realisation of how much I resonated with masculine energy.

Both are required. As women, we need masculine energy to get things done, just as men need feminine energy to be able to connect to others and relate to them. This is why the yin yang image is so powerful. Balance and the natural order require both, otherwise imbalance occurs and we are left with a world like it is today.

To further clarify why this is such an important subject matter, imagine this. The world and everything in it is a very false-masculine world, and we live in it in this way. If you have determined you're a feminine woman and you live in this world, the likelihood is most of your life is run on an inherently masculine basis, even if you feel like you are in touch with your feminine energy. If you have a professional or corporate life, the likelihood is all your work is very much modelled and lived in the masculine space, and often, when you have downtime, all you want to do is relax, chill out, or sleep.

Our lives are devoid of living in our feminine energy for the very reason our world doesn't support it. In developed countries, motherhood and childbearing and childrearing are still seen as an inconvenience, especially in the workplace. Although change is in the air for men and women, the modes of working have not kept up with what our multidimensional lives now need.

It is also, I believe, one of the biggest reasons that women doubt themselves. I still am unable to get over how many women over my career—hundreds, if not thousands—have shared with me, even when they are successful, how doubt is the most significant challenge in their lives, especially when it comes to their professional lives. They feel like they never stop asking whether they are good enough. Go back to step 3, and you can now start piecing together the various components feeding into our not-enoughness.

When the model of the world and the model of success are based on the opposite of who you are, when doing is the yardstick by how your worthiness is measured, how on earth can a core of being and feeling ever compete?

This is why I believe women doubt themselves. Our core of being and feeling is completely negated in favour of doing; therefore, of course we doubt whether anything we *do* is ever good enough.

So, what does this mean on our journey to be able to ask for what we want? It means until we can own our authentic power source, live from it in every aspect, and begin helping the world change to the extent there is balance between masculine and feminine so we all win, we will continue to try to play a game we can't really hope to win. All the while we perpetuate what isn't working, and are not helping to pave the way for change for our newer feminine and masculine generations to come.

But most of all we are losing out in being and living as the powerful feminine women we are, in all our glory, giving the gifts we came to give. Whether you're an executive or executive assistant, if you're not living and being from your core, you're short-changing yourself and the world.

Isn't it time for a change for all of us?

If you'd like to journal your journey using the *Six Steps to Six Figures Vision Book* and access the exercise pertaining to this chapter, please visit www.highvaluewoman.org/sstsfvisionbook and submit your details. You will be given immediate access. Enjoy!

CHAPTER 26

Cultivating the Lost Art of Being a Feminine Woman

Now that you know what your core energy is, let's get to the heart and soul of what it really means to be a feminine woman and how it can make a significant difference in your ability to ask for what you want.

One thing I admit I was quite ambivalent about when it came to this topic when I first started getting into it was the idea that being feminine meant wearing flowery dresses, etc. I'm embarrassed now to think that I ever imagined being a feminine woman was about anything as superficial as that. What I found interesting, and which made me smile, was how many women admitted they too had a horror of such a notion.

Our discussions led us to realise that just as we have the false masculine, we also have the "superficial feminine." This is the way feminine women have been portrayed in society, and an excellent documentary by Seibel Newsome called *Miss Representation* shows how this superficial feminine model of a very dangerous, one-dimensional view of women is shown in the media, thereby continuing to strengthen an untrue idea through almost unlimited channels and mediums.

In fact, embracing, owning, and living our true, powerful, feminine energy, once I finally understood what it really meant, humbled me and made me feel deeply grateful that I had finally found my way to my truth.

Living a powerfully feminine and energetic life is understanding that at your core, you *are* the power that creates worlds, and most importantly, it is inherent within you and doesn't require you to truly do anything. This is a profound statement.

Think about it. Whether you choose to be a mother or not, as a woman, we have the physical power to create lives with help from the masculine and give birth to it through the very vessels we live in. Everything about us speaks of power—our physical bodies, our glorious creative minds, our enormous hearts, and our boundless spirits. Yet throughout the ages we have allowed ourselves to be bound and gagged and made to feel less than we are for who we innately are. Being female became something we carried around like an affliction, not too dissimilar to the religious edict of Eve's curse.

I could talk about this forever. For now, I'd like to share with you how you can change your life by applying one single strategy that will reunite you to your feminine core like super glue and change how you live for the better. You'll be amazed at its ultimate simplicity.

In our current, very driven, and very false-masculine world, we tend to think it's all the doing that gets us real results. Many spiritual teachers have spoken of the principle I'm about to share with you, so I'm not talking about anything new; however, what I have learned from applying this principle and strategy in my life and for my clients is how it takes us into the heart of being a feminine woman.

The principle and strategy is the "be-do-have" paradigm.

We are currently living the "do-have-be" and "have-do-be" paradigms. This means we believe by *doing* (do), we *get* the things we want (have), and then we are whatever the *emotion* (be) we imagine we would experience by doing the thing and getting the result/outcome: "I do the hard work, get the success, and then I'll be content, at peace, etc."

The "have-do-be" is a variation of the "do-have-be" in which I believe that for me to be able to do something, I first must have something. Then after the doing, I will be … whatever I choose. An example of this would be, "I have to have the right background to get into the right school and be able to take the course I want to get the job I want, and then I'll be successful and happy."

This entire model is how the masculine world operates, as depicted in the definition in the previous chapter of the core aspect of masculine energy, which is doing. This is not to say it's wrong; simply to say if you're not masculine in your core, then this way of living will ultimately not fulfil you, and as we see for men who are masculine in their core, which is most them, this way works for them very well.

Therefore, if you're a feminine woman, imagine if you turned this principle on its head and lived it, as I am recommending.

Be-Do-Have

Being (be) is all about who you are in your core, what you choose to consciously embody, allowing yourself to experience this about yourself and for others to experience you in this way too.

For example, for me a way of being is to approach everything from a place of deep trust. *To* be *trust.* To know deep in every part of me that no matter what happens, everything is working out exactly as it's meant to be. This means living when things don't go my way with a sense of strong peace and being able to move forward far faster than if I have a belief other than what I have.

From this place of conscious *being* we act (do) based on who we choose to be, and we experience and create this experience of our self for others. This means our action is based on our core beliefs, aligned to what we truly know to be true, and therefore, when we act, our actions come from a place of profound integration and alignment. Not a simple ragged, knee-jerk reaction to something that happened. We know who we are, and we respond from this place every time.

This is then how our results and outcomes manifest (have) as a declaration of who we are and who we choose to be. Regardless of the results or outcomes created, when we live consciously and from a place of high awareness of who we are and what we do, we are experienced in this way, and this is what creates compelling charisma.

This is the true gift of authentic leadership, and for women, it's a way to tap into the magnificence of who we are in all our glory and live it in such fullness, we stand out from the crowd in all aspects of our lives. We love women (and men) who seem to just do their thing and create outstanding results, and they make no apology for who they are.

To recap, *being* is the starting point for everything and creates the space for us to consider our doing. Our *doing* is then powerfully focused, and action from this place is about who we are, as much as what we do; it's not coming from a place of fear, lack of confidence or incongruence. We're not doing for the sake of doing. We are aligned, intentional, and deeply authentic.

In turn, our doing creates the true *results* we choose, aligned to who we are and what we believe in, our purpose for being.

This is a philosophy that can change lives and is changing the lives of many women who start this journey as they realise this one key element. As feminine women, doing *must* originate from a place of being for it to pack the power it can. This is how we innately live as women. We fulfil ourselves when we allow ourselves to *be* and then do, and we drain ourselves when we constantly *do* without a thought of who we are being.

How many of you, regardless of what is in your lives, can feel the truth of that statement? I hope you can. It will change how you live.

If you'd like to journal your journey using the *Six Steps to Six Figures Vision Book* and access the exercise pertaining to this chapter, please visit www.highvaluewoman.org/sstsfvisionbook and submit your details. You will be given immediate access. Enjoy!

CHAPTER 27

Feminine Energy and Leadership— You Are a Leader

I'm going to spend some more time talking about feminine energy, what it really means for us as women, and why it's critical to live from this space if we are feminine in our core.

When we become very clear about who we are, what it means to be us, why we believe we are here, and what we want to create, having a plan that fulfils every part of us in our lives in an authentic and congruent way, especially exemplifying our feminine energy, means many things.

First and foremost, it means we have the power and energy to live this way and keep living it physically, mentally, emotionally, and spiritually.

Physically we begin incorporating physical practices that allow us to tap into the power of our female body to nurture, nourish, cherish, and love it deeply. I don't know what this might be for you. For me this means choosing exercise regimes that connect me to my body and its surroundings. Therefore, as much as I love working out, I equally love taking long walks outdoors. It means eating beautifully cooked, fresh, wholesome foods and indulging every now and then. It means loving physical and sensual experiences, from the touch of a loved one, to laughing out loud, to being around beauty in any shape or form. When I think about all the ways I can revel in being physical, the opportunities are endless. When I am physically fit, I have the energy to do all I choose to do.

Mentally for me means devouring books, movies, documentaries, museums, galleries, exhibitions—you name them, I love them. Anything that makes me think makes me feel alive, and I become like a dog with a bone. Growing my mental faculties has been a passion since childhood, and although it was originally borne out of a passionate desire to do and succeed, now it comes from a place of being deeply curious about how everything works and how I can utilise this knowledge within myself, transform it, and make a difference in the world.

Emotionally living a fulfilled life is about seeing everyone as a part of me, and I, a part of them in such a way, it continuously fills up my heart with love and compassion rather than intolerance or blame. It means standing in my power, teaching people how I would like to be treated, and keeping my heart open, so when I am working with others, my proclivity is to ensure I create win-win scenarios. When as feminine women we allow our hearts to be open rather than closed, we can create outcomes and results that take us into the realms of true leadership, irrespective of where you work and what you do, as most of our work involves people. Feminine energy is about relationships and connections, and when our professional lives operate from this space, lives becomes very different. We focus on true collaboration, not merely teamwork.

Spiritually, I simply spend time in daily practices like meditation and yoga to still my crazy mind and to remember and reconnect with who I truly believe myself to be. Taking time to cultivate the voice and power within means I hear her the loudest and more than every other voice. This is not arrogance; a fear many women have. It is simply a knowingness of myself holistically. This is my touchpoint to beginning each day. It is gratitude, intention, and then focused action to accomplish what I choose.

When we live as powerful, feminine woman, it means we have a guiding philosophy that works for us and helps steer us in this mad, gorgeous world we live in. When we know our true north and can simply move in its direction, we don't need to check in with anyone or anything. We are the wisdom we seek and pay heed to.

When we live this way, we gather to ourselves the people who will share this journey with us, and they become the people we need to share this journey with, because the likelihood is they haven't come into our lives by accident. I believe in a cooperative and loving universe, even when it's being very inconvenient and not being that way at all, and often for me, the people who have challenged me the most have also taught me the most.

Most importantly, by living this way we become leaders, even if we never aspired to being one. We may not consider ourselves leaders, but if anyone listens to us, asks us for our opinions, shares their thoughts with us, at some level we have become leaders, and the more we live in our power, the more we notice how people gravitate to us.

This is because there is a marked shortage of truly powerful, feminine leaders, and this is one area we need to change. Feminine leadership is required now more than ever, to ensure we don't completely lose our connection to all that exists that we are very much in danger of doing so, when we look at our world. Now, more than ever, we must find a way to balance the aggressive false masculine with the powerful feminine and masculine, and help women and men be who they really are, not just a horribly distorted version of our true selves.

We also need to help women reclaim their feminine power, so generation after generation of females are not born inherently considering themselves unworthy. This is the real tragedy of not living our powerful, feminine model. We forget who we are and why we are here. We have an integral part to play, no less than our masculine counterparts.

Our journeys are different, and yet the same. We're all here to reclaim our feminine power, heal the divine feminine within, live and give our gift, and partake of all the goodness the universe offers. It has been our disconnection and diminishment of the feminine that has us living the way we now live, so I ask you, "Are you ready to live the way you were meant and born to? Strong in your authentic feminine voice and power so you shine like a beacon for all other women and men too?"

When we step into this space, we radiate the divine feminine energy—the energy of the goddess—within us, and this is what gives us our true beauty. Not cosmetics or gorgeous clothes (as much as I love them!) This is an inner light that shines bright and true, and is the light of the divine feminine. Women long for it, men are drawn to it, and when we embody and live it, I promise you, heaven on earth is not an unrealistic expression of the life you might live.

If you'd like to journal your journey using the *Six Steps to Six Figures Vision Book* and access the exercise pertaining to this chapter, please visit www.highvaluewoman.org/sstsfvisionbook and submit your details. You will be given immediate access. Enjoy!

CHAPTER 28

What Happens When You Embrace the Powerful, Feminine Leader Within?

There is a consequence to all of this embodying our powerful, feminine energy and living from it, and it's one I was delighted to find myself enveloped in, like the biggest bear hug you could ever receive.

Imagine it.

You've uncovered who you really are, and you now know yourself to be more powerful than you ever imagined. All the things you've loved, liked, been indifferent to, disliked, maybe even hated about you—all of them are you, and you can see how, because they have all shaped you and made you who you are, you now love them.

All the characteristics, personality traits, and attributes that have helped you create the success and failures you've had, again you've realised they're all yours and they serve you, and so again, you love them.

Your foibles—the tendencies you imagined were annoying, worrisome, and possibly even tedious—you now see as integral parts of you, creating the multifaceted jewel, the diamond you are, and now when you look at yourself from every angle, you see your deep, sparkling, luminous, and radiant beauty.

The skills, experiences, opportunities, and mistakes you've lived and own all now show up in the perfect design of you, a knowing that no matter who might have skills and experiences such as yours, no one will ever live them like you, and in this moment, you finally grasp the truth. You have no competition. You never did, and you never will.

Everything, *everything* in your life up to this moment, in some way or another, has served you, and even though you may not have realised it, you own them too. They made you who you are, and now who you choose to be is much greater. The door of the infinite has opened, and you see the truth.

You are the indescribable, unlimited, inimitable, and infinite.

What do you imagine happens when you begin to see yourself in this way?

You fall in love with yourself. Truly.

You see who you are in all your glory, warts and all, and you love her for it.

We are not meant to be perfect. We are not meant to do things perfectly. We are not meant to have perfect things.

We came to embody our powerful, feminine truth in whatever way we deem it to be, and by living and giving it, we empower others to be and do the same.

When you see for yourself that this is who you are, you don't become arrogant, greedy, or aggressive. You see your place and the place of everything in the world, and your one aim becomes to make it better for yourself, others, and everyone.

This is the space we all aspire to occupy, and as women who find their place, purpose, and passion in the world, this is your home.

This journey will have you fall in love with yourself, as you have been, as you are, and as you will be. You will come to know there is never a moment when who you are and what you're doing is ever incorrect or wrong, and with this certainty, confidence, and compelling charisma, you will take your rightful place in the world and no longer shirk from asking for what you want. You have been the instigator and creator of it from the start. You will simply be claiming your just and rightful reward for living and giving your gift for the benefit of all concerned.

How does that sound as a basis to asking for what you want?

If you'd like to journal your journey using the *Six Steps to Six Figures Vision Book* and access the exercise pertaining to this chapter, please visit www.highvaluewoman.org/sstsfvisionbook and submit your details. You will be given immediate access. Enjoy!

CHAPTER 29

Finding Your Powerful, Feminine Voice

Thus far the journey has been quite an internal journey, and we're getting nearer to steps 5 and 6, where we will be taking all you have learned, created, remembered, and assimilated and turning it into solid action. For now, we will begin by getting a little bit more external than we have been.

This is the time to start taking all of who you are becoming and sharing it with the world, and the first step is to talk about yourself, as the woman you are and the woman you dream of and intend on being.

When you talk about yourself using what you already know about who you are and what you've done, and you can speak of this with certainty, confidence, and your brand of compelling charisma, this is when it becomes truly exciting! Stepping into the woman you dream of being, speaking the words that echo who she is through all your being, sharing her words from your mouth, based on who you already are—this is when your power starts to shine, yet it can be quite daunting.

Start small. Start with friends and family. Practice with personal tasks, challenges. Need to have a brave conversation with a friend or partner? Choose something that makes you a little nervous, and stepping into who you are and who you choose to be, speak from your body, mind, heart, and soul and say the words you long to say. Speak with your power. Claim it and own it. Let you power and radiance carry the conversation from your depths, not just from your head.

Listen to the words you might hear back and respond from the powerful, feminine place of who you are and who you choose to be. Let them experience you as you dream of being experienced, and when you find your fear showing up, remember who you are, remind yourself to breathe, and remember who fear is: an opportunity to be more than you ever dreamed of being.

Watch how you transform and how others wonder who you are. Practice, play—whatever it takes—keep stepping into this space in your personal life. By the time we get to the professional playground, your power will astound.

From this space pay attention to what comes up for you. You are living now from a heightened space of awareness and consciousness, which means you're likely to notice far more than you have ever done. Don't be surprised if you hear comments about how different you are.

Remember: subtle and slow, and if who you're being and what you're doing is working for you, rather than being perturbed by the people around you and any comments they may make, let them go. Change is frightening for the hardiest of us, and change in our loved ones make us very nervous, even if the change is ultimately for the better for all of us. In the beginning, they may not see that. They'll just know you're changing, and it may make them anxious. From your place of power, let them in as much as you choose, and be patient with them and yourself.

This is the aim of this chapter—to allow you to slowly access your courage and begin taking her, your High Value Woman, out for a spin. You've been uncovering her, adding flesh to her bones. She is now as real as you or me, and now it's time to step into her shoes, her feet, legs, arms, torso, and head. You are her—she is you.

Sometimes the change within you once you step into her, claim her and own her is very subtle, and you're the only one who really notices. Perfect. Live her, as much as you can. Soon what you will notice and what is most exciting, is when the world reflects to you who you are being. Things start moving the way you might want them to. People might start behaving the way you'd love them to, and even when they don't, you're okay with it. You stay, and reside in you and your power.

Use the work, the exercises you've been sharing with your journal, especially the "be-do-have" exercises from earlier. We will be using them much more in step 5, but for now, just take some little test drives with what you've been living and remembering. Utilise them in who you're being. Make sure you never act until you check in with yourself first as to who you want to be. After being whatever it is you choose, make notes about the outcomes.

Experimentation is the name of this game, and beginning to speak your power is the aim. Play with it as much as you can. The more you practice with various scenarios in your life, especially with situations that may make you a little tremulous, the more confident and congruent you will be come. By the time you're having those conversations with your manager, you'll have found ways of keeping those pesky butterflies out of your tummy.

If you'd like to journal your journey using the *Six Steps to Six Figures Vision Book* and access the exercise pertaining to this chapter, please visit www.highvaluewoman.org/sstsfvisionbook and submit your details. You will be given immediate access. Enjoy!

CHAPTER 30

Allowing Yourself to Receive (the Powerful, Feminine Way)

We've now reached the end of step 4, and you should have a strong idea of who you choose to be, having used all you learned in steps 1 to 3 to chart the way for you. Step 5 will continue in the same vein, but when you get to step 6, the information will require you to apply everything you've learned about yourself to create the professional results you now choose.

I hope you realise, as we continue this journey, that asking for the money, promotion, or opportunities in your professional life that you desire and choose is much more than just about the money. It's about claiming your birthright, your place, and your power as a woman, and the physical outcome of money is simply a reflection of who you have become. This is when you intuitively know that when you live in this space, the opportunities seem to find their way to you.

The power you own and live demonstrates to the universe that you value your gifts and are living and sharing them with the world. Whether you ascribe to the notion of the universe being made up ultimately of energy or not, what I have come to know for sure is this energy of pure power, passion, and purpose sends countless vibrations out, and before you know it, people and circumstances find themselves in exactly the right pattern for you to receive what you want.

My dearest hope for any woman reading this book is for her to come to know herself for the magnificent, powerful feminine woman she is, and in reaching this realisation deep within herself and feeling its potency within can finally live and gift her gift in the fullest manner possible. In doing so, she sets herself up for one of the biggest gifts she could receive (although her ability to be this recipient is the topic of the last chapter in this step).

We have been conditioned from our collective and individual histories to deny our power and magnificence, and in the process we have lost the ability, and in some cases our capacity, to receive. When the inherent, perpetual, and insidious message is you're not worthy, the smallest kindness appears to be a blessing, yet in our conditioned unworthiness or not-enoughness, we refute the blessing, less the giver may be tainted by our unworthiness.

This may seem a little unkind, and for some overdramatic, yet over my career I have watched woman after woman deny the assistance she has been offered because she believed assistance meant others thought she was incapable. And when woman after woman hesitates to ask for what they want and deserve, and conversation after conversation points to this core not-enoughness as the basis of every fear that stops us *all* in our tracks, the connections start to become clear.

To be able to receive the big dreams of our lives, we must believe we are worthy and ready to receive them with every part of us. To be able to receive the big gifts fully, we must be able to receive the smaller gifts fully, yet how often have we been unable to receive?

For me it's been a painful yet profound and moving journey to reach the point where I am now receptive to receiving with every part of me. There are moments when I forget, and the minute I do and I become consciously aware of it, I apologise in spirit, give gratitude for the offer I missed, and resolve to be and do better next time.

So how do you know if you are good at receiving and whether you will receive the big dreams of your life?

How well do you receive all that is offered to you now?

How well do you say yes when someone offers to help you? Or do you imagine he or she thinks you incompetent or incapable, so in your indignation, you say no and miss out?

How well do you receive compliments or gifts, especially from your partner? Did you know that when a man offers anything to you, he's offering part of himself, and in your denial, you deny him? This action can cut him to the bone.

How often do you allow yourself to receive the smile or hug from your children to the extent you feel the love they have for you, from within their tiny frames, all the way into your heart? From a loved one?

How often do you allow strangers to be of assistance, be it sheltering you from the rain, opening the door for you, letting you go before them in a line, smiling at you?

How often do you see and experience the moments of life that are a gift being given to you, so that one day, after being the grateful and loving recipient of all of this, suddenly you will receive the big dreams of your life, and your whole being will burst open in deep gratitude and love?

We don't often live this way. I know when I realised my capacity to receive the little things was determining my capacity not only to receive the big things but to receive them in such a way I felt the love in the gift of them. It completely changed my approach in receiving gifts.

When we allow ourselves to receive this way, we find the juiciness in the promotion, the opportunity, the raise. We experience the fullness of the dream, and we are inspired to be and do more, so we can have a deeper professional life and impact more people, make more of a difference.

In learning to receive little and often, the slices of soul in our everyday lives, we create the energy of being the recipient of the bigger gifts and dreams coming our way, and we teach the people in our lives how much their gifts mean to us and how they too can receive fully and beautifully.

And then something magical happens.

You not only learn to receive the good with love and grace, you learn to receive the not-so-good—and in the moment you do, you remember who you really are, the power within you, and suddenly the not-so-good doesn't have the power over you that you imagined it did.

When we receive, we tell the universe we appreciate the gifts it has sent us, and we know we are worthy of them. And in our deep, known worthiness, we let the universe know we will love and appreciate even more.

We all love the people in our lives who behave as if the gift we have given them is exactly what they wanted, and in their love for us, we feel the love we have for them, and we're more inclined to give them more gifts than the people who barely glance at our gift, or who struggle to say thank you, or even negate the gift in some way. This behaviour makes us shut down, so what do you imagine the universe does when you behave this way?

Learning to receive is the equivalent of saying, "Open sesame" in your career to being able to ask for what you want. When you ask and receive, you suddenly get better and better at being able to ask and receive.

This knowing and living your worthiness is another of the keys to the kingdom. Being able to receive, say thank you, and know more is on the way.

The gates are open. Will you let it all in?

If you'd like to journal your journey using the *Six Steps to Six Figures Vision Book* and access the exercise pertaining to this chapter, please visit www.highvaluewoman.org/sstsfvisionbook and submit your details. You will be given immediate access. Enjoy!

Step 5: Connecting to and Becoming the High Value Woman You Are

You now know who you are. You have chosen her. Now is the time to really embody her in all aspects of yourself to ensure she and you become one.

Embodiment is about taking what we have uncovered and remembered, deciding to focus on it, and create powerful momentum to truly live from this space and create a strategic plan for our professional lives that will reap all we desire and choose. We will know then we are living and being this.

Similar to formulating and cementing any new habits, new practices must be applied and lived consistently and often; we fall off the bandwagon because we're not feeling the sensations of these new practices as being who we truly are. This takes time, and in step 5, our focus will be on cultivating the following key practices so we set ourselves up to win each time, every time.

❖ *In the space of new being, our mantra for ourselves is **compassion**. This is the time where more than ever we're being kind and caring to ourselves and allowing our imperfections to shine through. This is what will create long-lasting change.*

❖ ***Progress**, not perfection, is our aim. When we begin moving into the doing, it will be about moving forward, not aiming for perfection. Perfection is boring. It's not messy, wild, making our hearts thunder in our chest. This is progress. Aim for progress.*

❖ *In the midst of it all we want to be **present**. Living in the moment, practicing the art of mindfulness, being fully engaged is what creates that strong sense of charisma. When we are present, we exude charisma.*

'Courage is like a muscle. We strengthen it with use.'
—Actress Ruth Gordon

CHAPTER 31

The Seat of Feminine Power— Emotions and Energy

The purpose of step 5 is to provide you with principles, philosophies, strategies, and tools to take what you have uncovered in step 4 and begin making the changes in your life at a holistic level. Everything you will learn in this book can be applied to the basis of your life, for we want the building blocks of our lives to be for all of life, not just professionally. This is what will make you a whole, aligned, and congruent woman.

One of the biggest challenges for women making this journey and embracing their powerful feminine energy is in the utilisation of one of our most potent assets—living with and managing the broad spectrum of emotions that we have access to and which, we have been told the expression of is inappropriate. Often, we hear how emotional women are, a supposed reason for why women previously weren't allowed to vote or be educated. It's due to this label and belief that we've tried to take emotions out of things and have sadly embraced the masculine essence of trying to transcend emotion.

This doesn't work for us if we are, in our core, a feminine woman. It asks us to go against the grain of our very nature—our ability to feel and relate to one and another, and to be and do it well—and when we live this way, we feel cut off from our core. Many women tell me how they find it hard at times to know and experience what they're really feeling, because they've been told they're too emotional, and in receiving this feedback, they made believe it wrong to feel the emotions they feel.

Our emotions are one of the most powerful tools we as women (and men) have been given, as a compass of who we are being in every moment of every day, and how we are being experienced by others. They also allow us to navigate the journey of our lives. This is probably a simplistic way of expressing this, but when we feel so-called positive emotions, the likelihood is we are on the right track. When we feel so-called negative emotions, the likelihood is we're not on track, which is why we're not feeling good.

Our ability to manage and use our emotions is our most powerful gift as women. When we detach ourselves from emotions because the patriarchal, false-masculine world we live in tells us it's not appropriate—the reason they say this, in truth, is that it's the one thing they're unable to manage and deal with themselves—then we continue to live a model that negates us and in the long term serves no one.

Everything ultimately serves us, if we choose to see it that way. Therefore, when we access and live our power, we give permission for others to be and do the same. I love hearing about the reconnection boys and men are making to their true authentic masculine power, and we need to be and do the same so we can meet each other in the divine, powerful form we were meant to have from the beginning.

Emotions let us know we're alive. When we experience joy, passion, happiness, and love, we feel invincible. When we experience fear, disconnect, sadness, and pain, we still know we're alive, because we're *feeling* the emotions, and it's those feelings that allow us to move out of them when they hurt or stay in them when they don't.

When people don't feel, they experience depression—a state that has the power to sap us of energy—and ultimately take us on the journey where we may lose the will to live. Not feeling emotions equates to being utterly disconnected from life to the point we welcome death. Death is a part of life, but death while we're still living is a state that, when experienced, can feel like oblivion.

This is why, when we don't allow ourselves to experience emotions, we feel powerless and find ourselves lacking in energy.

As feminine women, emotions feed us and give us energy. Have you ever noticed, when you are in a state of powerful, positive emotion, you feel as if you could take on the world, and when you're in a negative state of emotion, even getting dressed can seem exhausting?

This is, as one of my favourite teachers Neale Donald Walsch in his "Conversations with God" books has talked about; the alignment between energy and emotions. Emotions are energy in motion. I love this description.

Now you can begin to see how, when we don't allow ourselves to experience emotions, we subconsciously feel out of touch and not at all in our power, and we don't truly understand why. We're trying to live a model that is in its core the opposite of who we are. Does it make sense now why women are experiencing the loss of their power in every way imaginable?

It's time to own one of our biggest powers—our ability to feel and relate—to the extent we can change our world and the world around us. In the professional world, our ability and capacity to inspire people gives us the opportunity to be the leaders we dream of being, and it allows others to become the leaders they want to be. For those who choose to follow, the have something meaningful to be part of.

Meaningful work can create passion, drive, and a desire to excel and can be more than anyone can dream of—this is what people seek in the world today—in every sphere of life. When we as women can be this kind of leader in our personal and professional lives, this is what will change the world.

Our ability to authentically connect and collaborate reaps significantly large rewards, as we see when we experience it in the world in the truest sense. When we let go of fear, insecurity and jealousy; when we see the bigger picture and how it can benefit everyone concerned; when we tap into the emotions that will allow others to feel the vision too; this is the power to create worlds. It is the possibly dormant power residing within us that is ready to burn if we simply have the courage to unleash it.

Living this way, making no apology for being this woman, this is why you're making this journey. When we attach high energy to the emotions we want to embody (whatever they may be for you—remember chapter 23), this is what makes us shine. Our radiance emanates out further than we can ever imagine, and we effortlessly draw all that we choose to us. Isn't that what you want? Isn't that how you want to be and do?

Throughout step 5 we will talk about how you can live this way on a practical, day-to-day level, and you will learn processes that will allow you to know exactly where you're at in relation to your emotions, and how those emotions tie into where your energy is.

Emotions + Energy = Feminine Power

We will also look at what can happen when we don't live from our power and end up being at the mercy of our emotions. This is a state that doesn't serve anyone, least of all us, and has the power to unravel all we intended. This is not a place I choose for you, and hopefully, once you have an awareness of it, you too won't choose to live here.

If you'd like to journal your journey using the *Six Steps to Six Figures Vision Book* and access the exercise pertaining to this chapter, please visit www.highvaluewoman.org/sstsfvisionbook and submit your details. You will be given immediate access. Enjoy!

CHAPTER 32

Teaching People How to Treat You

Earlier I talked about how as you make this journey, the likelihood is you'll experience change, and as you change, the people around you will notice, which may make some uncomfortable. There is a reason for this.

When change occurs in any aspect of our lives and the lives of the people around us, it creates uncertainty, and uncertainty can be disconcerting if not downright scary. Tony Robbins often talks about the six human needs, two of which are certainty and uncertainty. We need both to live fulfilled lives, and one of Tony's most profound lessons, which I took on the day I heard it, has changed my life forever and for good. He said, "The level of uncertainty you can live with will determine the quality of your life."

What he meant was, ironically, the more I can be certain and comfortable about uncertainty when it shows up in my life, the higher my quality of life will be. This is because, unlike most people, when change and uncertainty come into my life, instead of perceiving it as a negative, as many people do, I approach it with curiosity and enthusiasm, like a small child.

For myself, I added another level. Not only do I approach it with curiosity and enthusiasm, I see all change as opportunities, the chance to be even more than I dream of. In fact, you could say for me, Fear = Opportunity, offering another chance to grow.

So why bring this up now? No doubt you will have noticed, as you change, the people around you also change. Some will like this new change, some will not. Some will not like it, and they will try to tell you you're a worse person for it. This is when tapping into your core, checking in with who you believe yourself to be is critical. You will know intuitively the people who will continue to be part of your journey and those who will not. When it comes to family, the challenge becomes exercising patience, compassion, and most of all love, when the people who say they love you may at times not seem very loving.

Why does this happen? In your changing, you alter the playing field for them, and now they feel like they no longer know the rules. To them it feels like the ground has been pulled from beneath them. For those who like to set the rules, it's even worse. Now, when it comes to you, they are no longer setting the rules—you are setting your own rules—what does that mean to them?

This is an anxious thought for many people who seek to control life and all that's in it. In the past, this gave them certainty. This is an impossible task—we all know—yet for the people who live this way, this becomes almost a matter of life and death, and they will fight you as you seek to change. In your power, they might be experiencing their powerlessness.

So how do we continue to live life and manage the illusory "fallout" of our change?

Simple. We do what Dr. Wayne Dyer has suggested: "We teach people how to treat us."

Have you ever noticed when you let someone know with deep love, respect, and compassion—because you see him or her clearly for who the person is—that you will no longer tolerate a particular behaviour? If you no longer play that game, he or she can't either.

This is not an easy principle, but it is a simple one. When you know your worth as a human being, you slowly begin to know the worth of everyone. This is when platitudes such as "we are all one" begin to formulate within you in a way that means something, and in time you come to realise that people can only behave poorly with you *if you allow or enable them to.*

As I changed, the people around me seemed to change. My most profound change came from my family. After spending so long trying to fit in and hopelessly failing, by simply being myself and making no apology for it, plus choosing to live in deep love, respect, and compassion for myself and others, my argumentative nature and desire to prove myself right slowly diminished, and I could be in a space of love, joy, and curiosity with everyone around me.

This is not to say people don't irritate me. I'm human, and so are they! I simply do my utmost not to react with the ferocity I used to. Now I aim to see them as part of me and with their own struggles, which from my own journey I know are not easy to overcome, whatever they may be.

Teaching people how to treat you in all aspects of your life, including in your professional life, means knowing your worth no matter what station others hold in life. They are no better or worse than you. Allowing a manager to treat you poorly, for example, reflects badly on you and the manager, and when you allow another person to get away with this behaviour, your worth takes a battering (as does his or hers, who just doesn't know it). But more so, the emotional and energetic aftershocks resonate out much further than you can imagine. Plus, you allow the perpetuation of that action to continue and become true for both.

Change, deep profound change that we need to happen in this world given where we are, cannot and will not happen if we don't challenge the smaller injustices of life. If right now you're thinking this is far more than a book about how to receive more money, well then firstly, I'm glad, and secondly, let me ask you this: Do you want your daughter, niece, sister, cousin, or friend to have to experience what you have? Don't we all deserve it to be better? If not now, when?

Teaching people how to treat you resonates in an ever-expanding circle, more than you can ever imagine. When you make a change and either stop or start a behaviour, you not only change your life, you change the life of the person who interacted with you. Whether he or she sees it that way is not your concern. You being true to yourself in deep respect, compassion, and love for all is all that's required of you. Some people may change, some may not. You are only responsible for your change and who you choose to be. They will respond now to *this*.

Help people be better than they can imagine themselves to be. Find ways to speak your truth in a way that resonates your profound respect, compassion, and love for yourself that in every moment is reaching onward, upward, and all around, and when this starts to reach them, watch how it changes them too.

What are some practical ways of teaching people how to treat you?

Check out the exercises in the vision book (link below) for how to change the way people interact with you forever!

You can access the exercise pertaining to this chapter by going to the link below and in the vision book, going to the relevant chapter. Please visit www.highvaluewoman.org/sstsfvisionbook and submit your details. You will be given immediate access. Enjoy!

CHAPTER 33

Boundaries and Non-Negotiables

Previously, we talked about embodying the characteristics and attributes you choose for yourself, as part of the process of uncovering the woman you dream and intend on being, plus the values that are important to you. These two items, together with the last chapter, have been setting you on the path of knowing who you are and who you choose to be, what's important to you, and how you decide people will treat you in all your life.

To bring this together, we're now going to look at an area most women find challenging, which perfectly ties into the next chapter. We can know who we are and who we choose to be. We can know what's important to us and live it. We can teach people how to treat us, and as a final step in this series of processes, we are going to create boundaries and non-negotiables. Without them, all of this can be for naught if we don't have a line we choose not to cross.

Definitions might be a good idea here, just in case there's any confusion between the two terms I'm using. Boundaries define the limits of what we will or won't tolerate. Non-negotiables are the deal-breakers. Obviously, these vary in personal and professional situations, and I would recommend you know what these are for you in both categories. In your personal life, define these even further for the various groups of people you interact with, as they may be different for your partner, parents, children, friends, and acquaintances

Boundaries and non-negotiables create the framework in which all the above live and is the space where we hold the consequences and implications of non-cooperation. In my experience, one of the biggest reasons for conflict in a professional environment often occurs when we don't hold others responsible or accountable for their actions and/ or meeting agreed expectations, and then get upset that they didn't cooperate.

The first time we let anyone off the hook, which can be as simple as not approaching the subject when it happens, we teach that our word and actions equal little or nothing. When we allow the behaviour to continue, not only do we lose credibility; we lose respect in our and their eyes, and in the eyes of anyone else around who saw what occurred.

Often, it's a subconscious process and one that can also happen in personal relationships. When it does, we're left wondering why our conversations always seem to end in defensive and sometimes conflict-ridden tones. By creating boundaries and non-negotiables, and communicating them from the start, or if we're already in a relationship (be it a partner or manager), drawing a line in the sand and asking to create some clarity for both of us, we set expectations of how we both want to be treated, and what the consequences and ways forward are, if either of us contravenes our agreements.

We don't hammer our boundaries and non-negotiables out all at once when we've figured out what they are. We may choose to have this conversation with our partner, because we've noticed we seem to get the wrong end of the stick at times whenever we have a discussion. Or maybe with your manager, the next time you realise neither of you are getting out of your working relationship what either of you want, these are perfect opportunities to recast the die and reset expectations.

Both ways, you determine (as with everything) how this will work for you and how you will communicate what this now means to you.

Defining our boundaries and non-negotiables is critical. If we don't know where we will draw the line, we might never do it; and slowly, our sense of worth will diminish, and we won't even know what happened.

This is the ultimate last nail in the coffin for our sense of worth. We will have allowed others to treat us poorly and in allowing this behaviour, communicated that it's okay for them to be and do so, because if we don't see our value and worth, why on earth would they?

In knowing who we are, what we value and how we will allow people to treat us, there will be lines they can't cross and if they do—manager, colleague, partner, friend—whoever they may be, there will be consequences, and we will hold them to this in the same manner as we expect them to hold us to.

And we will live this way because we love, respect, like, and value ourselves and them. In this sublime cycle, we increase our worth and the worth of the people around us.

Isn't this worth being and doing?

If you'd like to journal your journey using the *Six Steps to Six Figures Vision Book* and access the exercise pertaining to this chapter, please visit www.highvaluewoman.org/sstsfvisionbook and submit your details. You will be given immediate access. Enjoy!

CHAPTER 34

How Do You Be That? Living the Power of Being on a Daily Basis

I'd like to share with you a way of living the power of being by using your emotions. This is a compelling strategy, and one that has reaped me big rewards, deepened my relationships, and focused and centred me in my core—my heart centre—in a way I'd never experienced before. It truly has the power to transform your life if you will allow it to.

As feminine women, our ability to relate and connect is a natural source of our power, and it comes from many aspects of us, including our biology, chemistry, and physiology. It's something we do without truly having to think about it, but the more we've brought into the success model of the false-masculine world, the less we've allowed ourselves to be this way naturally in all parts of our lives, not just professionally.

It's particularly wreaked havoc in our intimate relationships, where women have taken on more masculine personas, and men a more feminine persona, and while there's nothing wrong in this, as I said earlier, if we consistently live a model that is not our core, we're unfulfilled and we run on empty. Therefore, as powerful, feminine women we must find ways to fill ourselves up in our natural energetic approaches, and one of the ways we can be and do this is by reconnecting to our strongest compass—our emotions.

By reconnecting ourselves to our emotions, firstly we gain a big insight into where we are for ourselves, and we begin listening to what our true self, our intuition, is telling us. That way we don't need to look outside ourselves for the answers. External validation can only take you so far, and it can drive you crazy if everyone is giving you different answers!

Secondly, when we reconnect to our emotions, we release our ability to feel again, and this is deeply powerful. For a long time, I lived my life intellectually, and as satisfying as that was, it was nowhere near as fulfilling as when I allowed my heart to get into the act. Suddenly I really did feel like superwoman. I had super powers—powers of emotion—that allowed me to tap into what others were feeling as much as I was, and I loved it when my ability to empathise wasn't simply an intellectual exercise. I felt what others were feeling, and a result of this my relationships deepened, creating a level of joy I hadn't experienced. And this was in my professional life too!

Thirdly, when we reconnect to our emotions, we also reconnect to our ability to be fully sensory beings. As women, sensuality is a large part of who we are. Living through our senses, especially when you haven't been, can be a delight. Remembering all our senses can remind us that life is not just about mental gymnastics. It's also about seeing, hearing, touching, smelling, and tasting; and when we re-engage all of us once again—body, mind, heart, and spirit—this is where all our life is, waiting for us to come back and *be*.

The tapestry of richness in feeling and experiencing emotions within ourselves, and then extending this courtesy to others, allows us, if we choose, when we are in a challenging situation with others, to step into their shoes, feel what they are feeling, and maybe even gain an inkling as to why they are feeling this way. We may realise their reaction to us has nothing to do with us, and it's in moments like these when we take the focus off ourselves and onto others that we allow ourselves to become the women and leaders we dream of being.

Emotions serve a purpose and provide messages for us and everyone else. We've forgotten this during occasional lapses of hysteria, and we often throw the baby out with the bathwater. If you're surrounded by people, wouldn't it be worth it each time to give yourself a moment to check in with how you're feeling before you speak? By taking this moment for yourself, you give the other this opportunity too. This split-second moment of checking-in can be the difference between a sublime or indignant conversation and subsequent result and outcome.

Positive emotions can also generate high energy, giving us the vitality to be and do all we need. We've all noticed how very uninspired we are when we aren't feeling positive and like our true selves, so it isn't simply that emotions are a guidance system. They also power us to move forward in whichever endeavour we choose.

What is the strategy for managing our emotions to the extent we live all the above at a much higher level than we have ever before, making a difference in our lives and the lives of everyone around us?

Simple. We make our emotional state our first priority—who we are being—before we say anything, take any action, with the intention of creating the outcome or result we want, from a space of high conscious awareness and capacity.

This is the be-do-have paradigm in action, and it is a simple strategy. It's also a two-part process: one to help us get into state and manage *our* emotions, the other an opportunity to step into another's shoes and experience what he or she is really feeling. Please use the link below to access the vision book online to complete the exercises.

For now, I will give you a further insight to what "being" is really about. Being is about being aware in all situations and consciously choosing the state of emotion you want to experience throughout that interaction. It's about making a decision to be strategic in your conversations and action items. Rather than simply tackling your mountainous to-do lists every day, it's about asking the question, first and foremost, "Who do I choose to *be* as I go about my day, interact with the people I do, take care of what needs to be taken care of, and do what needs to be done?"

It's about asking which emotions show you the truth of who you are, who you choose to be, and how you choose to embody them. It's about taking a moment to decide how your experience will be and feel. It's about being the creator of your world and not just a participant—all unwillingly at times. When we decide who we will be, how we will feel, and how we want to be experienced, we step into our core, determine what we want the reality of our day to be, and then look at what needs to be done. We decide how it will be done with intention, focus, and feeling, and from this space, our to-do list may change.

We are not working harder or smarter. We're *being* smarter.

If you'd like to journal your journey using the *Six Steps to Six Figures Vision Book* and access the exercise pertaining to this chapter, please visit www.highvaluewoman.org/sstsfvisionbook and submit your details. You will be given immediate access. Enjoy!

CHAPTER 35

The Dark Side of Emotions—Staying Centred in Your Core

This chapter is about what can happen if we don't manage and utilise our emotions from our core space of feminine power, to be of service to ourselves and others, for the betterment of all, in all aspects of our lives. It's an impact that reverberates not only for us as individual women but as a collective sisterhood of women, and civilisation as a whole. That's a big statement, I know.

It's also an impact that to my mind has been used as the basis of a false premise that in our not too dim and distant past (and in some cases, continues to be in parts of the world), the reason women couldn't be educated, take part in politics and commerce, hold office, or be able to vote, to name a few. Likewise, its paler shade of assertion—that women are still in some way considered inferior—even now exists in many insidious forms of misogynistic behaviour and can often be found very much alive and kicking in some corporate cultures. For most people, it's a nonsensical notion, yet it has been used as a weapon against us as women, and in its wake, has left the devastating effect of leaching away our power, our individual and collective feminine power, and the world has been a sorrier place for it.

What is this dark spectre I speak of?

It's a two-fold peril and one that is the opposite of what we've been talking about. At its core, it's when we allow the source of our power for good (our emotions) to become the source of power for darkness.

Now before you think you've dropped into a very poor version of *Star Wars*, hear me out.

How often have you heard some version of "women are too emotional"?

My guess is many a time throughout your life, and if you're anything like me, before you understood what it truly meant, you either reacted in anger or frustration (thereby perpetuating their belief and solidifying their experience of us as women). Or you became even more masculine, even more disconnected from your source of power, simply to prove "them" wrong. Either way, we lost, and lost out.

It's a subconscious, deeply treacherous, all-pervading cultural myth; perpetuated and dogmatised in belief generation after generation, transcending borders of every kind, saying one thing and one thing only: women do not and cannot possess what it takes to be of value in this world. It's done through one of the most prolific paradigms we've ever known, of women being unable to control their emotions. It's a belief that has broken the backs of women and one we are still fighting to this day.

Where has this come from, and what does it mean for us on this journey?

Where it's from is a sufficiently long enough history about the journey of women and our feminine power. I talked about author Riane Eisler (I highly recommend her books,) to understand how we landed in our current very dominant patriarchal culture. It will open your eyes.

For now, let's focus on how we can ensure we're not helping to perpetuate a myth that has only one basis for its existence—to keep us in bondage, away from the source of our power.

The way in which our power, our emotions, can be turned around and used as weapons against us are, as I said, two-fold and hold risk for us individually and collectively.

The first is when we live with our emotions in such a manner that we are at the control and mercy of them, and in this way, we simply react rather than pause to think through and then respond.

Please don't get me wrong. I'm not saying men don't behave in this way; of course they do. It's simply that it's not a charge you hear often levelled at men, is it? "Oh, men are just too emotional!" Yet even if you're a woman who's never lost it, the first time you ever do, it's what people may seek to remember of you, and in some cases, use against you.

The aftermath of this kind of behaviour is that once we have unleashed from a space of pure reaction, we may refuse to take any responsibility or accountability for how we behaved, citing the other as the cause of our behaviour, as if we had nothing to do with any of it, and it all came or happened because of *them*.

One reason we may live in this way is when we are driven subconsciously from such a place of fear that we can't see the pattern we are living, and until something happens to wake us up, we can end up living out the rest of our lives in this manner. This is a very common phenomenon and usually very correctable, if the person wishes it to be.

However, first and foremost we must be aware of it and understand the consequences of this behaviour, not only for ourselves but also for women everywhere. This might appear unfair—you're being held ransom for your fellow sisters—but how many times have we ever tarred men with the same brush when one man or some men behaved in a particular way? It's not fair, I agree, and it's a way of being I would love to see end.

The second is using our own or someone else's emotions, consciously or subconsciously through a process of manipulation and/or coercion, to get them to behave in a way that will create pleasure for us and pain for them, or simply not allowing them to make a conscious, aware decision in their interaction with us. We hide our true intentions, or simply choose to take advantage of others, especially emotionally, seeking the gain for us, uncaring about any loss for them at all. In this scenario, it's always about us.

This is an even darker use of emotion than the first way, as it seeks to take power from another, whereas in the first way it's simply a reaction, based on living a highly unaware life. Both can be utilised by men and women, but it's women who are more likely to be perceived as tainted by using it.

Being and living this way, and the behaviours that result, demean everyone concerned and put us in a place where none of us wins. Drama—tense and taut drama, mired in anxiety, stress, and fear that in the end exhausts, empties, and leaves us powerless in the process—is the outcome of using emotions this way.

For those of you who may imagine you don't know what this looks like, how often have you seen people fly off the handle because they simply reacted to something that was said or happened? Or saw people behave in a way where you unwittingly knew they were taking advantage of another?

These ways of being aren't hidden in society. Often, they are right in the open, and because of the significant rewards sometimes attached to behaviours that we may abhor in public but act out in private, we all in some way, shape, or form know what it looks like and feels to live in this way. When we're finally brave and honest enough to acknowledge that we have lived either in the first or second way, or even both, then we can decide whether to continue like this or choose differently.

The consequence I feel of living this way as an individual woman, and collectively among women, is that we undermine ourselves and each other, and nothing is more tragic than when I see women behaving this way toward each other when we run up the ladder of success and then pull it away; when we behave in a bitchy fashion to a woman we perceive is more attractive than us; when we judge another woman and try to one-up her; Or when we ultimately forget that the only reason anyone behaves in a negative way is because they are in deep pain.

A Course in Miracles says, "All attack is a cry for help."

When people, women or men, behave in any of the ways above, the likelihood is they are in pain. Some people are very aware of their pain, and because they can't cope or live with it, they fling it out of themselves onto others in the hope it might lessen theirs. Others have buried their pain deep, the mere thought of it having them react like a wounded animal. For some the pain has been wiped from their conscious lives, so they live in a "dead" state, yet they operate from their core of pain.

Wounds created in individuals in the depths of their sub consciousness, mired in the fears we talked about in step 3, are the perfect breeding ground for this kind of behaviour. Wounds in the deep collective unconscious, as Carl Jung talks about, is an even deeper topic and outside the scope of this book, but it all leads to one thing.

Who do you choose to be?

Do you choose to be a woman who uses her power, her innate and inherent ability to manage and utilise emotions—her power source—to connect and relate, so we can individually and collectively be better? Or do you choose to be a woman who will use her source of power to get what she wants and damn the rest?

This is a choice you make, and it's not one I or anyone else is going to sit in judgement on, because since you've been reading this book, my guess is you want to be the woman you dream of, and you want to inspire the women and men around you and generations of females to come.

If this is what you choose, then choose to live a conscious and aware life for yourself and the people around you, and disarm those who would seek to use your power source against you.

Now that I feel like I've done my Xena, Warrior Princess bit, I'll finish with one last bit of advice.

There will be moments in your life where you may be called to access and utilise emotions that in the past you've never needed, and in those moments, you'll wonder whether it is right to do so.

I'm not a woman who gets angry—I admit I've been known to have a very, very long fuse. I can get annoyed or frustrated, but angry? Someone would really have to push my buttons.

The first time I was in a situation where I knew I had to establish a boundary (i.e. someone behaved in a way that had violated a core belief of mine), I had to respond in a way that would leave them in no doubt that this kind of behaviour would never be acceptable. They then could decide how they wanted to move forward. I knew where I stood.

To say I was frightened was an understatement. I knew if I didn't step consciously into my anger and speak the words I knew I had to say so this other party would "get it" (diplomacy was not going to work), I would no doubt have to deal with this situation again and again.

In a way, you could say I had no choice, but I don't believe in that premise. I had a choice as to how I would respond, and I chose to respond in justified anger, and although the party in question was very surprised and it changed our relationship forever, I was at peace with my decision.

The outcome of this exchange was that I never experienced this person in this manner again, and I heard on the grapevine that her perception of me was forever changed too. I don't know if it changed the way this person behaved with others; it changed the way she behaved with me, and that was all the outcome I was after at that stage. I was still young and didn't realise my actions had likely created a ripple effect.

In some scenarios, using what we class as negative emotions can be a powerful option, and it's one I believe we should all have in our tool box. Let's not be naïve, ladies; we've all had to deal with some challenging situations in the workplace and beyond.

Living in power, using the source of our power for good always, in all ways, may at times make us feel like superheroes, and why the hell not?

We are, and it's time we owned all the power inherent within us.

If you'd like to journal your journey using the *Six Steps to Six Figures Vision Book* and access the exercise pertaining to this chapter, please visit www.highvaluewoman.org/sstsfvisionbook and submit your details. You will be given immediate access. Enjoy!

CHAPTER 36

Number One through the Gift of Gratitude

Now that we've got that out of the way, and I can go back to being my sunny self, let's talk about making yourself number one, through the gift of gratitude.

I know the moment I make this comment there may be many women who subconsciously shudder and run for the hills or argue that as a wife, partner, mother, daughter, and sister—whatever role you wish to use—this cannot be.

And I must hold to my ardent beliefs and say, "It must be," and hope I can find a way to encourage you as to why it's integral to this journey you're on.

Making yourself number one does not equate to the height of selfishness, nor does it mean others are worse off when you do. It means you prioritise your needs and wants as part of the broader life you lead, which includes all the people and activities this entails. You know within yourself, if you consistently do not tend to your needs and wants, you will suffer for it, and everyone around you will too.

And how will you suffer? From a loss of your feminine power, energy, and life force, the very things that make you who you are, these core pillars of your power will drain away. As they say time after time in the planes when we fly, we must take care of our oxygen mask first before we can be of service and use to another.

Still, we struggle with this notion. We feel bad, guilty, less, to the extent we become ghosts of women with all our to-do lists for everyone and everything, but we—the powerhouse who makes it all happen—are empty, unfulfilled, and unsatisfied, and it shows.

When we live this way, our radiance dims, our light shines a little less brightly, our power wanes and eventually splutters and gives out. Ten, twenty years later, we wonder, *what happened?*

This is too common a story for it to continue, and too hazardous a precedent for what it means for our daughters, nieces, and generations of women to come.

We as women, to be able to live and give from our power, must see, behave, and live as immensely worthy beings in and of ourselves and find ways among all that we are and do to nurture, nourish, cherish, and love ourselves by giving ourselves what we need.

Why is this such a challenge to us, and what is a way of feeling like we're number one, without compromising anything and anyone in our lives?

My sister is my inspiration for this chapter. She is younger than me, married to one of the best men I know, mother to three gorgeous children, and is a business owner. Whenever I talk to her, I am amazed at how she and her husband still manage to laugh and tease each other, her children are a delight, and she is building a business, as well as sharing the responsibility with her husband for building a home for their family.

Yasmin and I talk usually every week, and she shares with me how she gives herself Saturday afternoon as often as she can, as "her time," time for herself alone to be and do as she pleases. In a week, the space of a few hours gives her the recharge time she needs, and even if she would like more, right now, this is what is working.

One of the lessons my sister taught me about the time she takes for herself is the basis of the strategy for this chapter, and one I use diligently every day. Yasmin taught me that one way she can make herself number one, not only in the time she has for herself but in every day of her life, is by practising the art of gratitude for herself and her life in a way that fills her up without needing any grand gestures. This is as simple as it sounds. Probably not as easy to implement … but I will leave that for you to decide.

By looking at our lives every day, with all their ups and downs, when we can view it all and be grateful for it now, I believe this creates the space to realise we must give ourselves this time. That way we can be grateful now and in the future, not only for what we have but what we will receive, and most importantly, for who we are.

Gratitude is one of the simplest tools in the tool box, yet it is by no means the easiest. Gratitude is not really gratitude when times are good. It's easy to be grateful when things are going well. It's gratitude when times are tough—especially when times are tough—that is key.

Gratitude is and can be the result of trust when things aren't going so well. If you can find within you through your belief about who you believe yourself to be in your core, the ability to trust, you *will* have reasons to be grateful, then the energy this sends out reinforces the notion that you will have something to be grateful for and creates it.

The ultimate reflection of real gratitude is gratitude for yourself, and this is how in your core, in your being, who you truly are, you make yourself number one in a way that fills you up and fills up the people around you. When the people who love you see you being grateful for *you,* and then grateful for everything else coming your way, they are inspired and in their subconscious inspiration behave in ways that support and nourish you.

How do you find ways to be grateful for yourself?

Maintain your centre through everything we have talked about so far. Focus your core through the simple gratitude of *you*—nothing else—just gratitude that you are alive, here and now, as you are and destined to live and give the life you came to live.

Start here, in the smallest ways possible, to be grateful for you and then branch out. Be grateful for who and what are in your life, all the blessings you can find each day, but make sure you start being grateful for yourself first and foremost. From here decide which small acts allow you to truly experience the gratitude you feel for yourself.

This is the gratitude my sister, Yasmin, experiences as she manages to take the couple of hours she may be lucky to get, and it's the lesson I'm hoping to experience too. I also hope, for those of you who may not have additional responsibilities of partners and children, that you too can give yourself the gift and not fall into the trap of feeling selfish or guilty, because you *can* give yourself this gift but may feel you shouldn't.

Whichever way this principle pans out for you—single and/or childless, connected and a parent, or any option in between—be and do this for yourself. It is through practices such as this that we can create a world where being grateful for ourselves, each other, and all will become as natural as breathing.

Thank you.

If you'd like to journal your journey using the *Six Steps to Six Figures Vision Book* and access the exercise pertaining to this chapter, please visit www.highvaluewoman.org/sstsfvisionbook and submit your details. You will be given immediate access. Enjoy!

CHAPTER 37

Being More, Doing Less

We're almost at the end of step 5, and soon the journey will be moving into what I call inspired action, which is the natural culmination to everything we've been talking about: the true art of asking for what you want with confidence, certainty, and charisma in a way that makes others want to give it to you today, tomorrow, and forevermore. Wouldn't that be nice?

Before we get to that, I want to mention a few last steps where I'm going to ask you to move even more into a space you may not have been occupying, a space that may go against the grain to everything you know and have lived.

I've said a few times we live in a false-masculine world, and all our models of success are based on this premise. Meaning if you're a feminine woman at your core, as successful as you may be, on some levels you're probably feeling drained and you might be finding yourself wondering, *Is this it?*

If you're not too many years in your career and already feel like you're working your fingers to the bone, as much as you want to scale the ladder of your dreams, part of you questions whether it's worth it.

If you're a way in, likely you're already feeling this way and you're wondering how you can make it better. How can you really experience the juiciness of your professional life?

And if you're fully in, you want to know how you can truly love the rest of your career life in a way that will fulfil your body, mind, heart, and soul. In fact, I'd say all of us are asking this. It's what makes us feel alive.

As feminine women, at our core, *doing*, the core descriptor of masculine energy, as important as it is—and it does have a part to play, as you will see in step 6—can't be the predominant way you interact with the world and leave your imprint on it. Why?

We started talking about this in an earlier chapter, and we're going to revisit it here.

If your doing is not driven from your *being*—the core descriptor of feminine energy—the person or people opposite you are not experiencing the truth of you, and in this we are all missing out.

As feminine women, *being* before we ever do has the power to create and change worlds, yet when we get caught up in doing, because this is the model and world we live in, we end up behaving like little mice on wheels: forever going around and around, never truly moving forward, tiring ourselves out, and then in the end, potentially dropping out of the rat race altogether.

There is a way to create the success, abundance, and holistic life you choose, and in this chapter, as we move into the concept of inspired action in step 6, I'd like to suggest a two-step process that can make a huge difference if you're willing to trust me and give it a go. It can be used in any personal or professional situation.

Firstly, decide you will live from your powerful feminine energy and space. Cultivate this in whatever way is right and true for you. What works for one of us may not be what works for others. Choose what is for you.

Next, focus on who you are, who you believe yourself to be, and who you want to be. You see her very clearly now, don't you?

Now from this space, choose the powerful emotional states you wish to embody, based on the previous statement, as you face whatever may be in front of you.

From this place, from a state of *power,* ask yourself, "What is it I must do? What is the action I must take?"

Asking for what your inspired action needs to be from deciding and determining who you are and who you choose to be means you give yourself the space to be and respond. You don't simply react or act without reflecting on what you are trying to create and why.

We all have twenty-fours in the day, and too many hours end up lived on autopilot due to the "things" in our lives. This is a sure-fire way to wake up one morning when we're old and grey and wonder where our lives disappeared to.

Once you've truly started living the "be-then do" paradigm (i.e. owning your feminine power and then taking masculine action), I'd like you to consider—just consider, mind you—what your life and the lives of the people around you would be like if you consciously and in full awareness decided to find ways of *being* much more and creating ways of doing less?

I'm not asking you to shirk any duties, obligations, or work. I'm merely suggesting there may be ways where in your life, if you were to take the time to fully *be* in your feminine power, you may find ways of being far more effective, efficient, and successful if you did less.

Just a thought.

At the end of the day it's not about working harder or smarter, it really is about *being* smarter and finding ways to live the juicy lives we dreamed of.

Aren't our dreams worth some reflecting time? I hope so.

If you'd like to journal your journey using the *Six Steps to Six Figures Vision Book* and access the exercise pertaining to this chapter, please visit www.highvaluewoman.org/sstsfvisionbook and submit your details. You will be given immediate access. Enjoy!

CHAPTER 38

Vulnerability and Transparency— the Real Power Tools

As we near the end of this step, there are a couple of final principles I'd like to share with you that have completely changed my life.

We hear a lot about the notion of vulnerability—how, when we show who we truly are, we live lives of authenticity and transparency. People experience us, not our masks. What I have come to know is that we're often not even aware of the many, many masks we are wearing, therefore getting to the core of us so we can truly be vulnerable and transparent may not be as easy as it sounds.

It is, however, a journey worth making, and one I would encourage you to take with every opportunity you receive. The more we delve into who we really are (steps 1 and 3) and then decide who we choose to be (steps 4 and 5), the more we must find the courage to live this truly. When you live this way, vulnerability and transparency aren't aspects of you to be or do, they become simply who you are.

If you're finding it difficult in your life to be vulnerable and transparent, the likely answer is you have beliefs that tell you that to be transparent and vulnerable is not a good idea for you. You may have had experiences when you have been honest and open and were negatively impacted or hurt to the point that you decided you would never allow anyone or anything to hurt you again. You put those boxing gloves on and found a way to fight for what you wanted, and you received it.

I know this scenario intimately. I've lived it for over forty years, until

I finally reached the point where I was physically, mentally, emotionally, and spiritually exhausted. I had created a life that was deemed highly successful, yet as we've discussed earlier, it didn't feel successful. In fact, it felt empty, and I wondered how it was possible to build a life that on the outside was the pinnacle of success yet on the inside was as hollow as a shell.

Eventually, through working with a coach, I identified the reason for my emptiness—I was living a wholly masculine life. My feminine energy was non-existent; it was wreaking havoc in my personal life, and most importantly, I was not at peace in any way. I wanted to take the boxing gloves off, yet I was petrified. I had no idea how to live where I didn't have to work harder than God, fight for everything I wanted, and not feel guilty for daring to sleep in on the weekend.

In the end, what I learned was I had to become brutally honest and transparent with myself. It was only when I could be completely honest to myself about myself, I could even begin to have honest conversations with others. I'd spent much of my life saying I was fine; I could cope; I'd find a way. The notion of saying, "I haven't a clue and please can you help me?" was even more terrifying than admitting I didn't know what to do.

Similar to the idea of learning how to receive, I finally learned how to ask for what I needed from other people, which demonstrated I needed help. My initial forays into sharing my vulnerability were worse than dreams of being caught naked. I felt utterly exposed in those conversations, and slowly, as I began to see the gift of my asking for help where the other could help me, I realised I had been doing a significant disservice to the people in my life who liked, respected, and loved me.

In my career, I started sharing when I didn't know the answer and asked for help. I stopped being afraid that I wouldn't be seen as an expert and trusted that in opening up, my relationships would deepen. They did. In being open and honest, I encouraged others to be and do the same. Some did, but many didn't. In their model of the world, asking for help or showing a lack of knowing was a weakness, and they wouldn't admit this. I learned for myself it was okay for all of this however it panned out, and I found a sense of peace I had not known.

We live out our entire lives with many masks, to the extent we sometimes we forget we're even wearing them. When the inner emptiness becomes too much to bear, we realise something is wrong, yet even then we are afraid to unmask. We don't know how we will be received.

In professional lives, we fear we may miss out on opportunities if we are vulnerable or transparent. Our work spaces don't engender either, fearing we will be manipulated into losing that which we dream of, or if we show all our cards. In the end, what moves us into the space of being vulnerable and transparent is our desire to be seen, heard, and experienced in the truth of our being.

It took time, and I am still on the journey, yet one thing I am sure of: I can't be a leader of any kind if I am not willing to be vulnerable and transparent with my life and everyone in it. I still have moments of abject fear, and in professional opportunities, it takes time to say what needs to be said, rather than agree with the crowd. I may not be liked for it. I may even miss out because of it, but what is true for me is if I must hide any part of who I am any more, this (whatever "this" may be) is not right for me.

I trust the voice within, the voice of my powerful feminine self that tells me I am more than enough no matter what is happening on the outside, and I believe this voice, and I do my best to live it. I know in my living this way I encourage those around me, and the people who choose this too slowly show up.

This is the greatest gift of these two power tools, and in the ever-increasing sublime cycle of a self-fulfilling prophecy, this is the space I choose to stay in.

In owning the truth of all of us and being able to live it, show it, and then share it, we remember the secret to owning our worth. We are all of it, and it is within.

If you'd like to journal your journey using the *Six Steps to Six Figures Vision Book* and access the exercise pertaining to this chapter, please visit www.highvaluewoman.org/sstsfvisionbook and submit your details. You will be given immediate access. Enjoy!

PART THREE

~Ask For What You Want ~

'We never know how high we are
Till we are called to rise;
And then if we are true to plan,
Our statures touch the skies.'

~Emily Dickinson~

Step 6: Filling Treasure Chests (Inside and Out)

We've talked a lot about being, becoming, and embodying. Now we're going to start creating some inspired action and tangible results, specifically getting the money, promotions, and opportunities into your pockets!

To truly create congruent, aligned, and deeply inspired action, you must be clear about who you are (we did this in the previous five steps), why you are choosing the work you're doing, and how the work you're doing is adding significant value to yourself, your manager, division, organisation (and for those of you that choose), and the world.

Wealth and abundance come to us first because of who we are and then because of what we do.

This is a critical statement and why almost 80 percent of this book and my coaching programs are focused on the being state, before we get to the "real" doing: feminine energy first and then masculine.

If you can't embody and articulate the magnificence you are, you are not being true to yourself, and true wealth and abundance can't find you. It's almost as if your signal to the universe (and to everyone and everything around you) is too weak to be picked up.

Time to step into your truth. Time to ask for what you want and deserve.

'Know Thyself.'
—Temple of Apollo at Delphi

CHAPTER 39

A Professional Life You Choose to Live and Lead In

After all the work we've done over the last five steps, we're now at the stage where we will begin moulding the clay of what we wish to create. This is where the deep clarity you now have about yourself can be mapped and aligned to all you have created and achieved, and you're going to take it to new heights. I know it because this is the journey I took, am still taking and likely will take all throughout my life. I've helped countless hundreds make it throughout my career and am now helping my clients undertake it for themselves, so they can reap the rewards they want and deserve.

This is the place where we have landed, and it's very exciting. It's a place where we really have the power to make our dreams come true. We started at the core of us; we branched out in our beauty, strength, and power; and now we come into our own.

The reason I find it so exciting is that my intuition tells me you're most likely already a successful woman, and you picked this book up because you felt there was something additionally you could learn. I hope with all my heart this is the case, and what you've discovered is your true source of power that will now allow you to live at a whole different level.

When I finally began living an authentic life, powered by my deep knowing of who I was, what I chose, and how I could finally live from my feminine energy and magnificence, I astounded myself with how success flew to me and how much I really began to love myself, my career, the people around me, and ultimately, all my life. I found the bliss Joseph Campbell, the author of *"The Power of Myth"* talks about that I'd been seeking.

The satisfaction and fulfilment I felt in my career went through the roof. I began interacting with everyone who encountered me with all I am, rather than censoring myself, imagining I needed to behave in a particular way, as deemed appropriate by the corporate world. I realised I'd been far too serious, and now my cheekiness, which seemed to endear people to me, became my calling card, and before I knew it every professional relationship deepened. I came to know the people I worked with, and they came to know me, and our results were created from a space of true respect, cooperation, and collaboration.

People long to be who they are in their work. They long to be seen, heard, experienced, and received. They want more than anything else to flourish, but we have allowed outdated and false norms to dictate what and how this ought to be, to the point that people and creativity are stifled, and no amount of values work and branding is going to change it (unless it touches the hearts of the people it is supposedly there for and sparks the creative and innovative genius we all go to work to unleash and explore).

As we make our way through the final step and the chapters in it, I'd like to start here with three overarching principles. These principles, along with all the inner work I do on a continuous basis, lifts me to realms of inspiration and passion in my work. These principles govern the essence of this step.

In the following chapters, we will go into a lot more detail around each as it becomes relevant. There's a lot more than meets the eye.

The three strategies are

❖ **Principle 1**—You must take ownership, responsibility, and accountability for everything to do with you in your professional life and career.

❖ **Principle 2**—You must develop a strategic approach to all aspects of your career and earning capacity by creating a strategic plan for your career (ensuring you incorporate your powerful and priceless vision).

❖ **Principle 3**—You must learn how to speak the true and authentic language of win-win through the formation of congruent and collaborative relationships, ensuring the focus is always on articulating the win for the other person *first*.

These are your new philosophies and strategies for the professional life you choose to lead, and it's one we lead with relish. It's why we're here, and it's our reason for living and giving our gift in the first place.

The world is filled with millions of people, including many, many women, creating success on their own terms, and it's time for us to rewrite the rules so women everywhere can succeed on their terms. For us to do this, as much as this is going to sound like a bad James Bond movie, we must firstly infiltrate the power structures that currently exist in our society that are still woefully light on female representation, and help them start making the change we know will benefit all.

I believe in cooperation and collaboration, and I've worked with enough outstanding men who are smart and wholehearted enough to know our current way isn't working, and we are ready for a change for the sake of all of us and future generations. I believe to start, this change must come from us as women being empowered individually through making journeys such as these, asking for what we want by creating powerful win-win scenarios, and then moving into those leadership roles, where we will have the power, with our fellow men, to make and live the changes we all need desperately.

This is my cunning plan.

So, ready to play with me?

I hope so.

If you'd like to journal your journey using the *Six Steps to Six Figures Vision Book* and access the exercise pertaining to this chapter, please visit www.highvaluewoman.org/sstsfvisionbook and submit your details. You will be given immediate access. Enjoy!

CHAPTER 40

Creating Truly Congruent and Authentic Relationships

Before we delve deeper into the understanding and application of the three strategies I mentioned in the previous chapter, I'd like to start with what I believe is the backbone of step 6, and the start of the rationale for principle 3: You must learn how to speak the true and authentic language of win-win through the formation of congruent and collaborative relationships, ensuring the focus is always on articulating the win for the other person first.

"No person is an island." The actual quote is "No man is an island," and I know you'll forgive me this one amendment. This is the start of a beautiful poem by sixteenth-century poet John Donne, which talks about the spiritual principle of "we are all one" from the perspective that whatever we do, whether we realise it, we impact another and all.

This may seem a tad philosophical for a book about how to receive more money, but given my belief that money is simply an energetic exchange of values between parties, I thought I'd mention it here. This to me is the golden rule: the way I have lived my life, and why I believe I have had the privilege and blessing to live such a successful and fulfilled life.

The basis of this chapter, then, is how I believe we must be and live as the kind of people we aspire and are inspired to be, in the knowing that how we treat others is ultimately how we treat ourselves and vice versa. The impact of these decisions and behaviours have the capacity to change lives.

I've watched people behave as if they are either inferior or superior to others, and there are many levels of this, something you will come to recognise far sooner than you imagine once you begin observing at the level of consciousness. We all behave in this way due to the society we live in, and we all live it to degrees in each category. I make these statements as observations, not judgements; I am as guilty as the next person in sometimes stepping into these patterns in my subconscious moments.

The challenge with being in this space is if we believe either notion with any sincerity, and of course, it is usually very subconscious within us as we would never dream of admitting either, we will behave in response to these ideas. Therefore, understanding the journey of our beliefs to the culmination of action and results is critical. The minute you experience yourself behaving this way, you can change it, should you wish to. You can change your beliefs about who you believe yourself to be, and who the other is to something that supports, sustains, and nourishes you in every sense of the body, mind, heart, and soul.

I spent most of my life believing myself to be inferior, and I've experienced many other women doing so too, and often it's due to beliefs we have about ourselves, others, and the world, and as we've already gone quite in depth into this, I won't go into it here. You can always go back to steps 1 and 3 for a refresher.

Therefore, let me ask you this. What would be a way of seeing others that would help you and the others to live in this world the way you both dream of? A way that would support, sustain, nourish, and help you both succeed? A way that would bring out the best in you both? A way where you could see the others—whether they are behaving "well" or "badly"—in a way that makes you grateful they exist?

Often, we despise and demonise the people who challenge us in small, medium, and large ways. They bring out the worst in us, and if we're not careful we can blame them for how we are being. Yet we all know we are the ones choosing how we are being, irrespective of the external circumstance.

Therefore, what if they aren't the monsters we imagine them to be? What if they are, as Tony Robbins calls them, "Your worthy opponent"? What if one or many others have come to help you become far better than you ever imagined or dreamed? And in the journey with you, whether you see it or not, they too become far more than they ever dreamed. Some of them will experience this journey. Others won't, and they won't thank you for it, either.

But if in the process of your journey some sage person helps you see how one or many others became the catalyst for you and your life becoming what you dreamed it to be, how will you see them then?

In my life, I have had the privilege to live in different countries, make many friends, and from those friends create family. Many were people I met professionally. Some I made the decision not to have in my life, and as I look back over the twenty plus years of my career, I can see how every one of them helped me become who I am, and for that I am eternally grateful. And yes, there are one or two I still grumble about, even though they helped me grow significantly!

When we see others as an integral part of our journey and us in theirs, even when we might not get on, we can utilise every experience to keep gaining opportunities to be and do who and what we choose. In every moment, this is all life is asking of us, and when the ones come along who really push our buttons? Well, let's just say we grow a lot!

We know this, and we forget this. But in remembering, we stay in our power and we remember who we *all* are. It is from here, this space of knowing and remembering who we are and who and how we choose to be, that we can be the leaders we want by demonstrating this in thought, word, and deed. From this space, building relationships is not just about us. It's as much about them, and our intention becomes wanting the best for them, as well as ourselves, and as many others as concerned.

There will be moments when we may need to be the fierce or arse-kicking feminine. We don't shy away from this space, because we do it from a place of respect, love, and a desire for them, just like us, to be better in every way. Again, they may not see it that way. We still choose to live from this space.

With all my teams, when I met them for the first time, I would set two main expectations for them. One, that we would have a lot of fun working together, but if I ever needed to kick their arse, I would lovingly; and two, if I was providing them with feedback, it would always be from a strong desire to help them be better. Of course, I always spoke to them individually to find out what that looked like, so we agreed in the way arses were kicked and feedback was given. And it was a two-way street. I expected them to be the same with me, and eventually they would very kindly oblige me once they realised I was serious.

I cherished the time I had with my teams, and I feel very blessed I still have beautiful friendships with many of the people I have managed. I'm also deeply happy with the relationships I created from my professional life that spilled over into my personal life, and for me, this was who and what I wanted to be: someone who creates powerful, devoted relationships that work both ways.

There will be always be people in the world who are deeply insecure and who may behave abominably and tell you you're naïve to think you can have such relationships in a professional capacity. Hogwash is what I say. You get to choose the kind of relationships you want to have, and you have the power to create them. If you choose to behave with the intention of believing as I do, that "no person is an island," then throughout your life you might find there is magic to be lived in the time we spend in the so-called professional world we live in.

As the Bible says, "Be and do unto others as you would have done unto you." I'm not a religious person, but it's not a bad way to be or live, I think. As always, it's your choice.

If you'd like to journal your journey using the *Six Steps to Six Figures Vision Book* and access the exercise pertaining to this chapter, please visit www.highvaluewoman.org/sstsfvisionbook and submit your details. You will be given immediate access. Enjoy!

CHAPTER 41

Creating an Inspired Plan with "P3" (Know Thyself)

The rest of this part of the book holds all the information you need to get yourself into a space where, as soon as you have read the numerous chapters coming your way, you can start applying what you've learned in your professional life.

You've done a lot of work already—congratulations—and now, all your work is going to turn into a tangible, strategic plan that starts with a concept I call P3.

What is that? I hear you ask!

I admit it. I was a huge *Charmed* fan, and when I created this concept, I named it P3, and you'll soon see why.

P3 stands for the practical foundations on how we will develop the three main strategies I talked about earlier on. The three main pillars of this concept are

❖ P1—preparation
❖ P2—practice
❖ P3—professionalism

These three principles will govern your application of the strategies, tactics, and tools you're going to learn. They are practical principles that require your active participation to gain the full benefit.

P1—Preparation is self-explanatory and will be covered in the next four chapters. The remaining pillars will be covered in the remaining chapters and will bring you to the culmination of your inspired plan and its implementation.

As with the rest of the process, this is a step-by-step journey, because nothing trips us up faster than not knowing what the next step is.

If, after you've read the book and while busy implementing you find yourself stuck in any way, you can find my contact details at the back. Please do get in touch. I'd love to help.

Now, let's get cracking!

P1—Preparation: Know Thyself

P1 is the start and will be the largest section, and no doubt you've guessed why. Like the rest of the book, the effort you put in is such that once you master it, you will live it, rather than it be something you keep doing. It will simply become part of the journey you take, and you will get better and start asking for bigger. This is my dream and prayer for you, and why P1 will set you (and others) up to win.

There are several facets to P1, and after each slice of content, to really help you get what you need, you will find "powerful practices." These practices are exercises that will ultimately become your strategic plan, so please take the time to do them as fully as possible.

The first component of P1 is about knowing ourselves from a professional perspective in such a way that we can articulate who we are and how we can add significant value with profound confidence, core certainty, and compelling charisma.

At the start of this step, I have used the ancient Greek saying of "Know thyself". It's a maxim that has been bandied about for a very long time in philosophy. It is the basis for a lot of personal development. Your work in steps 1 to 5 has brought you a long way, far further than many would experience, and your awareness of yourself is now required at the next level. *Being* now focuses and moves into *doing* and *inspired action*.

Knowing yourself at a professional level is the key in many ways for understanding what success and fulfilment mean to *you*, and the only way for you to know this is to intimately know who you are in this context and to be able to talk about it and yourself. Most women see this as selling themselves, and I know how much you all hate it. You tell me all the time!

I felt the same way. When I first started in my career, the idea of it for me at the beginning too was yucky, until I realised my belief behind it. Once I understood it's not "selling myself"—because no one could pay me my worth; it's about articulating the significant value I add—the yuckiness diminished.

Slowly I began to think of it as stepping into my power—owning it, knowing I am excellent in the delivery of it, and the outstanding execution of the delivery of my gift is reaping rewards.

Remember, you have no competition. You are unique. There is no one else at all exactly like you, therefore, no one is ever going to steal the job you want because your unique value proposition, *you*, is what it's all about. Therefore, P1 is all about solid preparation.

Most people, regardless of how many interviews or review meetings they have done, get nervous. The challenge is to communicate who you are in such a way that you do it beautifully, despite the nerves. You're going to speak as if you love the skin you're in because you absolutely do!

Who Are You? What Are Your Strengths/Areas for Improvement?

In my experience of twenty plus years of international HR and recruiting so many people I've lost count, when women are asked any form of this types of question—Why do you want this job, promotion, or opportunity?—they all share with me how, although they may have felt confident, inside was a deep, inner squirm that had the tendency to grow bigger the longer the meeting or interview went on until it reached a point where it began to impact them and their ability to be themselves and articulate their value.

I'd heard some form of this too often. It made me delve deeper, and what I learned from the women who were open enough to share it with me is that most of them, even with years of experience, balked at these questions. They disliked them with a passion, and in response I shared with them my experience of being on the other side of the table when they answered these dreaded questions.

I revealed to them, as I'm revealing to you now, how in the cases where the request or interview hadn't had a successful outcome, that after debriefing with the manager, the reason they were turned down was often because they didn't articulate strongly enough why they should receive what they asked for. Their value proposition didn't resound to the point of us saying, "Yes!"

Some of the feedback usually included overall language wasn't confident (even though they thought they had been); a struggle to articulate what they were good at due to a fear of bragging; a propensity to use the word we when it was clear it was really I; phrases such as "prove my worth" with an underlying perception of anxiety; and sometimes, as shocking as it may sound, a desire to take less than what was being offered that many managers would raise eyebrows over. Clearly, they couldn't understand such behaviour and it made them think twice!

When I share my experiences, women usually gasp and say, "No!" and I say, "Yes," and I believe it explains why the pay gap exists and why I became such an advocate for helping women get better at these conversations. In these scenarios, being on the other side of the table was frustrating, saddening, and on occasion, downright maddening!

This is why you're now going to partake of some exercises as a component of P1, as to how you can show someone who you are and what you can do with a healthy dose of confidence, a high level of certainty—because you own it—and your own personal brand of charisma.

❖ Powerful Practice: Get Those Gifts Out!

This is an exercise to help you begin getting strong clarity on who you are professionally with a holistic slant (always our approach) based on your strengths, weaknesses, and gifts.

Once you know your gifts, as before, be and do whatever you must to *own* them!

1. This is a two-step exercise. First, make a list to describe yourself. Put everything down, based on the roles you have in life (not just at work), and describe yourself in those roles. Write it all down.
2. Now, make another list of what you are good/excellent/ outstanding at. Again, refer to the roles that you play in your life and list all the things you would consider as strengths in those roles.
3. Once you've done that, think about and write down what you are not so good at and what you would like to improve in those roles.
4. Now think about the work you do. What are you good/excellent/ outstanding at in your work?
5. And next, what are you not so good at in the work you do, but you'd like to improve in?
6. Now, taking both lists together, how many of your qualities overlap? Look at your strengths and weaknesses and come up with one list for both.

By this point you should have a good list for both aspects of you. The reason I ask you to look at your life and work life and the roles you play is because there many skills people ignore because they don't think they're relevant.

For example, if you are the one in your group of friends who always organises events, outings, etc., but don't have much call to do that in your work, who's to say it's not a strength you couldn't list in an annual review meeting or job interview? For all you know you could find a way to utilise it in your current or a new role. It may sound trite, but it can reap big rewards.

So, go ahead and make the lists!

CHAPTER 42

Creating an Inspired Plan with P3 (Know Your Value)

Once you know where your strengths and gifts are, it's good to understand what the value is of the skills you have. It's also great to gain a deep appreciation of yourself as a person with those skills, and what you bring to the table possessing those skills not only in your work but in your life.

At this stage, we're not talking about the monetary value of those skills; this will come later. This is a simple statement of appreciating you as the person with those skills.

It's challenging to speak with conviction and certainty about your strengths, and show who you're talking to how great you really are if you don't believe this about yourself, deep within. We've done a lot of work in this space already in steps 1 to 5; therefore, this will be brief, and the powerful practice below will help even more.

Go into an interview or a pay review meeting and speak about your strengths from a deep place of appreciation, and the value you hold for yourself for having that strength, and believe me, you will stand out from the crowd.

Women like that are hard to forget.

❖ Powerful Practice: Shout Those Gifts Out!

1. From your list of skills and strengths, write down that skill or strength you really appreciate having. What value does it add to your life and the lives of the people around you? Make sure you write as much as you can about this for your personal and professional life, and if you can, really try to articulate the value, especially in your professional life.

2. To help you remember yourself with all these skills and what it feels like being this person, we're going to anchor all that appreciation into yourself, remembering all the times you demonstrated these skills and strengths and how amazing you felt. Remember them all now as vividly as you can, using all your senses.

3. Make a gesture that helps to remind you of all of this. Either clench your fist or touch a part of your body—anything that reminds you of how it feels.

4. In this way, the next time you're on an interview or at an annual pay review meeting and you've been asked that dreaded question, not only will you be able to answer it with confidence, passion, and certainty, you will feel great about it.

5. In the moment you're talking about it and feeling good, anchor it again doing the action you did previously. This will anchor it to you even more strongly so that every time you go for any kind of meeting, you will feel better and better and better.

Identifying Your Unique Selling Point (USP)

Getting very clear on who you are and how the skills you have bring value is critical to your success and fulfilment. It creates within you the knowledge you are appreciated and valued, and you're starting by being and doing it for yourself.

We're now going to take it a step further to help you get to really know who you are in this space, and we want to find out what it is about you that is special. Not special in the way everyone yearns to be but how you actually are because of you, your life, your experiences, your perspectives—everything.

This point will give you far more clarity once you have it, because at the end of the day there are many people who possess the skills you have, but there's something about each one of us that's unique.

If you can identify your uniqueness, it will give you an edge. This uniqueness is called your unique selling point.

So, what's yours?

This is not something you need to bang your head against a wall to try to figure out. It's quite a simple process. This is about *you*, so don't fret about whether your USP really is your USP!

❖ Powerful Practice: Special—That's What I Am!

1. From your skills and strengths that you listed previously, list your top three.
2. Why did you choose those? What makes them your top three?
3. What makes them special? What do you bring to the table that makes you unique?
4. Why would anyone value that about you?

Having a USP is not necessary, but understanding what is unique about you and the skills you possess helps you answer that dreaded question in an interview, "What makes you the best candidate for this job?" Or in a pay review meeting, "Why should we pay you more?"

Being confident about who you are and what differentiates you from the rest is a skill that can reap great rewards. And again, it doesn't matter if someone goes in and says exactly the same thing—it's the way you say it that matters.

Convey your USP with passion and certainty and you will believe it—and so will the person you're talking to.

I'd like to end with a couple of points I must mention before we move on.

First, the concepts of belief and faith as part of this process. If you don't believe what you're saying about yourself, it will show.

Congruency—the ability to align every aspect of you to what is true for you—speaks the loudest. If at any point you don't believe what you're saying, you are incongruent, and the manager or interviewer will pick up on it from your body language, your gestures, and your energy.

If throughout this process, you ever have a moment where you don't believe something you're telling yourself, find out why. Go back through steps 1, 3, 4, and 5 and work through your truth. You and your life deserve it.

Second, motive, and this one is simple. Never ask in fear. If you don't have the confidence of your convictions, if your being is not lined up with your actions and words, be and do whatever it takes to get you there and then ask. Again, go back through steps 1, 3, 4, and 5 and work through your truth. You will be better for it.

Now that we've confirmed your inner landscape, let's talk about the outer preparation we must do to ask for and receive what we desire and choose.

CHAPTER 43

Creating an Inspired Plan with P3 (Know Your Field and Industry)

Like any adventure, you need to know the lay of the land so you can cross it with confidence, certainty, and charisma!

What do I mean by that? When you're going for a new role or opportunity, most people will do research for a few reasons: to find out if this is the type of company they want to work for, whether the company will suit them, to get information to use at the interview, and several other reasons. For you to have an edge when you are part of this process, you will need a much broader frame of reference, as explained below.

Now that you know who you are, what you can do, and what kind of amazing value you can add in any situation, personal or professional, you need to understand where you fit regarding your field and industry. This is an integral part of being able to ask for the money you want. If you go on an interview, pay review meeting, or promotion discussion asking for a level of salary that's nowhere near your level of experience and skill (and believe me, many people do this), you lose all credibility and can be guaranteed to be on the pile marked "Thanks but no thanks!" You don't want this to happen to you.

There are many reasons you should be completely up to date with what is happening in your field and industry, and they're not necessarily only for the reasons I listed above.

My personal belief, and one that has stood me in good stead

throughout my career, is that your reasons for researching your field and industry must be aligned with what I share below. Given the work you've already done throughout this book; I know you'll understand why without my having to tell you.

❖ You have a genuine passion and desire to know what is happening so that you can excel in your field (and chosen industry)
   ▪ Many people in a job sometimes struggle to demonstrate what is really happening in the world and how that impacts what they're doing, or if they do, it's at a top level. Think about it. If you're up to speed with what's occurring in the world, you can think not only about how to manage your career but how to excel in your current role by analysing what is going on, applying it to you, and adding significant value. This is a way to create opportunities for yourself that don't yet exist. It's a strategy I have used time and time again very successfully.

   For example, in some of the most recent economic crises, many people understood there would be a tightening of belts and redundancies would abound. They saw them happening, and for many it was a time of fear and significant uncertainty. Not nice at all. Yet what did most people do in these times? They dwelt in fear, closed down even more, and tried to hold on as tightly as they could to what they had, reacting with fear when conversations happened as changes required them to. We all understand this and can empathise, but it's not where we want to live.

   A smallish population made the decision to start planning. They sent out resumes, built networks, brushed up on their skills, and continued to add value so that when they might have to move on, they wouldn't be too worried. Now, who from those two groups would you like to be?

   It's always good to be prepared and ahead of the crowd, not in the thick of it where you can't see anything that's happening. Other reasons for researching your field:

- You're able to demonstrate your knowledge of what's occurring by applying this knowledge to your field, industry, and specific work, thereby continuing to find ways of adding significant value;
  - You're then able to keep adding to your CV or performance review document what you have accomplished and how you have added value by keeping ahead of trends in your field and industry.

These are quite simple premises, but not many people do it.

Keep up-to-date with what's happening and have a genuine desire to understand what's going on from a much broader perspective and how you and the company you may be working for or with can either ride it out or benefit from it.

❖ **Powerful Practice: Checking In**

To get the low-down on what's occurring, you only need two things to start with and to continue with as you make it a regular practice. Weekly is best.

What you need are a couple of hours and access to the Internet. Google is my magic word. This or any other search engine is the best place to start.

1. Search both your field and industry and put in this year's date alongside the search term. This will bring up any references that you could possible need. Have a scan through and click and read any items that catch your attention.
2. From here, find other sources, either websites or publications that are a part of your industry, and make sure you subscribe to at least two or three.
3. Keep looking. Sign up to newsletter e-mails, online subscription pages, etc. You will be amazed at what you learn, and better still, after a week or two you'll start connecting the dots. That's

when your brain starts kicking into creative mode and you're no longer just part of the crowd.

4. Make it a regular practice and keep applying anything you're learning in the work you're doing, when you can. This is key. Many people keep up to date with what's happening in their field and industry, but very rarely actually apply their learning in their work. Stay up to date because it's who you are and what you do. That way when you do need to go for an interview or pay review meeting, you're not suddenly cramming, as if you were taking an exam.

If you're researching your industry, you'll get to know who the players are, and if you ever get to go for a meeting with one of them, it's easy to knock their socks off by having a better-than-average understanding not only of the industry but of their part in it.

Being in touch with what's going on will create additional passion, and it will stir you to know and do more. How good does it feel to know you're being and doing this to help you and others and in turn, this knowledge is going to keep helping you and them forever?

CHAPTER 44

Creating an Inspired Plan with P3 (Know the Salaries in Your Field and Industry Inside Out)

As well as getting to know your field and industry, you also want to know what the salary and earnings capacity is within them. There are many sources that will give you this information, and again one of the best places to start is Google. I promise, I don't have shares in Google!

In the time I have been in the reward and remuneration industry, I have seen the data available publicly grow exponentially, so it's quite amusing when a client says it's a struggle to find the information. I will share with you this information below, and from your perspective, it's simply about learning how to do this for yourself, and most importantly, be discerning in how you analyse and utilise it.

One of the easiest ways of finding out what kind of salaries and earning potentials are being offered in your field or industry is to search something like "salaries in (add your field)." As I said, you will be inundated with information, so you will need to be discerning. At the start, gather as much as you can, and slowly you will come to know which the better, more reliable sources are.

Start with the big job-hunting websites in your locality and then branch out. In the UK, some of the big ones include – www.totaljobs.com, www.indeed.co.uk, www.monster.co.uk, www.jobsite.co.uk. When I lived in Australia, some of the ones I used included – www.seek.com.au, www.mycareer.com.au, www.careerone.com.au. Forbes in the USA have also provided some good examples, including www.simplyhired.com, www.glassdoor.com, www.usajobs.com, and of course, no mention of career websites can miss out www.linkedin.com. Carry out searches for job websites in your city on Google and see what shows up. Many of them will offer some sort of salary references, either tables or graphs; salary centres; salary calculators; etc. so check these out.

Another way of using these websites is to scan through the jobs and review them and the corresponding salaries. Make comparisons between jobs and salaries. Some industries will pay more, some less depending on numerous variables, including what might be happening in your economy locally, nationally, and globally. Be thorough in your research, and make sure you're looking at your field specifically, and then look at what is being paid in the various industries for your field.

Fields are usually broken down even further, allowing you to be much more specific; however, general field salary information will give you a wider range. You may also come across salary surveys provided by recruitment agencies and other companies. These are very useful and will often give you an idea of the range of salaries being paid.

Any surveys that are provided for free will obviously not be as useful as a paid survey, but getting access to a paid survey is unlikely (unless you work in remuneration). The free surveys gather their data from a few sources, such as through ads that are being run, or collation of information where it was requested from various data collection methods, including pages where people put in what they are being paid, etc.

The reason they are free and the others are paid is that paid surveys are generally completed by companies and the data collected is based on strict criteria, thereby making it a challenge to contribute and access if you don't fit the specific criteria. This information is what the companies are paying, and the subsequent data that comes out in reports is far more accurate. They are based on actual salary data, so the data is considered far more robust. Free surveys are generally not based on actual company data.

My personal advice to you is to take the job sites and free salary surveys as a good guide and keep researching your field and industry.

Clarity with Salary

Before we get into the nitty-gritty about salary and the value of you in your role, let's be very clear what salary means to you.

Many companies are now adopting or have already adopted some form of the "total package" mind-set. This means that as well as salary, there may be other components of pay plus a bonus, or a car etc. so if someone offers you a $100,000 package, this does not necessarily mean a $100,000 salary.

In some countries, for example, Australia, companies add superannuation (pension) at a percentage to give a package amount. Therefore, if the superannuation percentage was 9.25 percent, then the actual salary component in the $100,000 example would only be $100,000/1.0925, or $91,533.

If anyone at any stage of any conversations about salary starts talking about salary, package, reward, or remuneration and you don't know what they're talking about, pause and gently ask them what they mean. It's better to have done the research in salary in your field as advised above and know what you are discussing than be caught out later. Also, as many companies have global, regional, and local hubs, language can become confusing, so clarify if you need to.

Additional items like bonuses, cars and any other kind of package items are usually considered in addition to the basic salary. Therefore, make sure you're clear around the numbers. You don't want to come away thinking you've negotiated a $100,000 *salary* when in fact you've got yourself a $100,000 *package*!

Know the Value of Your Role in Your Field and Industry

Now that you know what your industry is paying, how can you find out your value within your field and industry? That way, when you go in to ask for and negotiate your salary either in a current or new role, you come out with what you want.

Most people make the mistake of assuming this is about what they are worth, and you know my thoughts on the concepts of worth and value. In truth, this is about what you are valued at, with the skills and experience you have in your industry at this point in time.

And it's about what the companies and organisations can afford and choose to pay! This is perhaps the most integral sentence you will read in this whole program when it comes to salary and earning capacity.

There are exceptions to this rule, and believe me, they are exceptions. And likely, all I am teaching you may make you an exception, as you will be far more prepared than you have been before. However, at some point in the negotiation, a company may genuinely say, "We can't afford that," or some semblance of a similar statement.

It does happen and it's happened to me, so there is one point you must always remember. Let it become your mantra.

Companies have salary budgets. If you as a candidate or employee stand out and the manager or interviewer is prepared to pay over their budget or pay you more and maybe allocate less to another role (it does happen), then you have become an exception. Remember—to be an exception; you need to be exceptional and stand out, and all that I am teaching you will help you to be and do just that!

How can you get a good idea of your value in your current role in your field and industry based on the skills and experiences you have and where you would like to be?

You're used to me now. It's a simple exercise!

❖ Powerful Practice: What's My Number?

As I mentioned above, compare jobs and salary and earning capacities of those jobs.

1. Pull as many job advertisements in your field as you can, and print them out and read them. Do this with about ten to fifteen jobs (or as many good comparisons as you can find—the market may be slow) across the full spectrum of your field. The jobs will be from all sorts of companies, so you will also get an idea of which industries pay better than others.

2. After studying the jobs, compile the ones that you feel represent where you are and where you want to be in the next two to five years.

3. Make sure you're being honest about your current skill level. Don't up-sell yourself if you've picked a job that you aspire you to and you don't have at least 70 percent of the skills or experience required for that job.

   a. Are you where you thought you would be, remuneration wise? Are you surprised?

4. When you look at the roles you aspire to be in within the next two to five years and the associated remuneration, how do you feel about the number?

5. And finally, when you look at these aspirational roles and the skills they require, if you don't currently have them, what will it take to get them?

Another strategy you could use is setting up alerts from the various job sites of your current and aspirational role. That way you don't actively have to do the research—it comes to you!

Industries fluctuate based on the economy and what is happening in the world, so nothing is in stone. Therefore, after a financial bust, when we're booming again and people have worked hard and added significant value, they will renegotiate. For right now, however, you should have an idea of what the market will pay you for your skills and experience.

In the next section I will teach you a tip about how to increase your value by using the skills you have or skills you can learn.

What Are "Hot Skills" in Your Field, and How Can You Make Sure You Have Them?

One way to guarantee a higher level of salary and to continue in the vein of passionate, purposeful development and progression is to possess something called "hot skills."

Sometimes your specific niche in your industry can be a hot skill.

Other times, within your role, you can already possess hot skills or learn them to make yourself more attractive to the market, and below is a way for you to do just that.

❖ Powerful Practice: How Hot Am I?

By now you will have a lot of information about your field, industry, and salary within those spheres.

1. From your research, you will have a good idea of where your field and industry are moving and the kind of skills that will be required going forward. Compare this research with the jobs you looked at. What stands out? Where is the trend? What skills are prevalent in the jobs you looked at? What's happening to the economy locally, nationally, and globally?
2. If you possess those skills, make sure you're talking about yourself based on those skills and the significant value you've added, being in possession of those skills. If you don't, find out how you can get those skills. Either take a course or find a mentor who could teach and coach you, or you may even be able to learn these in your current role.
3. Continue to identify hot skills and keep putting yourself at the top of the pile. Act in the direction of gaining those skills, but never say you have a skill or are doing a course if you haven't signed up for it. (Again, this has happened!)

Now that you have a real depth of understanding regarding your field, industry, and salary practices in those areas, it's time to put everything into a plan of action. But before we get to that, one final word.

Putting Yourself in the Space to Succeed

We're now at the end of P1, and I know you're thinking: *What? We're only at the end of P1? P2 and P3 are still to come!*

Fret not, you'll love it!

Saying that, look how much you've already accomplished—how much better you know yourself, your skills, and your value. Plus, you are now sufficiently armed with information about your field and industry.

To finish off in this space of preparation, and to give you an idea of whether you are where you think you are, below is a checklist of questions you might consider asking in this preparatory stage if you're unsure:

- ❖ Am I ready?
- ❖ Do I feel like the High Value Woman I know I am?
- ❖ Do I believe in me/what I am saying?
- ❖ Do I have answers?
- ❖ Am I as prepared as I can be?
- ❖ Can I successfully articulate my case?
- ❖ How am I "being"?
- ❖ Am I attached to my outcomes, and if so, how can I detach myself?
- ❖ How will this be for all of us?
- ❖ How will I be if I don't get what I ask for?
- ❖ Am I ready? (Repeated intentionally.)

CHAPTER 45

How to Ask; Strategy 1: Start by Having a Strategic Plan for Your Career

You'll have seen from the last few chapters that this process starts before you ever really think about having the conversation with your manager or an interviewer!

The reason for this, as you've no doubt gathered, is in order for you to be able to speak confidently and articulate the true value of you—your skills, experience, in fact, all of you—you must first know, experience, and feel it deep within you. Then when you speak, your power and magnificence flow out as an expression of you, ready to gift the world.

This is why, at this stage, I will share with you ten powerful strategies for helping to get your manager to yes when it comes to asking for and receiving the pay raise, promotion, or opportunity you want, and how you move forward if for any reason the answer is no. The way you behave in this scenario is in fact even more important than how you behave through most of these strategies, so please remember this.

These strategies can be used if you're not in a role and are only at the interview stage, but you will need to select the steps that are relevant to you in that process, and then of course apply the rest of the strategies once you land a role. And fear not, I will go into detail a little later about having those pesky interview conversations.

We're now going to use everything you've learned and begin delving into a more methodical manner of applying all I am teaching you. Technically we're still in P1, but you'll see very soon, the "conversation" starts before you ever make your actual request, helping the P2 stage, practice, to be utilised efficiently and effectively with the very person you'll be making the request of.

The ten strategies to helping you get your manager to a yes (and how to manage a no) begins with the understanding that it all starts far sooner than you imagine.

Strategy 1—Have a Strategic Plan for Your Career

The key message for this first strategy is, if this whole process starts before you ever actually ask your manager anything, then it makes sense to realise in a way that this is a never-ending process that begins from the minute you start your very first role to the day you retire from your career.

How is this possible?

Simple. It's the utilisation of principle 2, which I talked about in chapter 39, which states you must develop a strategic approach to all aspects of your career and earning capacity by creating a strategic plan.

What I mean by that is if you understand that your career is a strategic plan, you must aim to have as much clarity as you can about everything concerning your professional life, including your earning capacity before you go for any interviews or sit down with your manager and start talking about pay raises.

I'm not saying you have to have a hundred-point plan, complete with dates, timelines, action items, etc. (you can if you want), but we all know what happens when we're too structured—we experience tunnel vision and are unable to see the wood for the trees.

No, what I mean is this. Know what your ultimate outcomes are for you career in these three main areas and create a working strategy that changes and grows as you do. The three areas are:

❖ Career development (how you will grow, learn and change);

❖ Career progression (the ladder of your choice you will scale); and

❖ Your earning capacity and potential (the lovely dollars/pounds and other goodies that will come your way because you ask for them).

Developing the ability to always have strong clarity on why you're in the career you've chosen, how you want to develop and progress, and ensuring you're keeping abreast of how remuneration is tracking in your field, your industry, and the economy as a whole is critical in managing your career and earning capacity.

Once you have worked through what the above three look like for you, remember this one powerful truth: make sure whichever company or organisation you decide to work for is a fit for you. This is where you're going to be for the next few months or years. You do this by interviewing them as much as they interview you. If you're already in a role, never fear. Start from where you are and simply be mindful of it now or the next time you go for an interview.

For those of you who may be in some stage of a recruitment process, please apply the above rule in your recruitment process. Far too many people place all the power of selection in the hands of the interviewer/manager/panel, and in doing so, we, especially women, forget our own value and the significant difference we can make in the role in which we're interviewing. It's also an important aspect for you at a personal level when you're doing your research that the organisation fits into your beliefs and values.

When you demonstrate this ability of interviewing them as much as they interview you, something happens. It's a subconscious process, and likely one worth utilising in every aspect of your lives, especially relationships! Not only do you begin to own your worth and value, the people in front of you, on the other side of the table, do too.

Another excellent outcome of this approach is that you might actually uncover something that makes you think twice about taking the role. Questions about the things that are important to you, phrased elegantly and in a strong context, are impressive and convey a sense of discernment that from my experience of twenty plus years of interviewing, managing, and coaching people lets your potential future or current manager know who you are and how the two of you will interact.

If it works, this can be a match made in heaven. I have had maybe two managers in my entire career I didn't enjoy my time with. All the others propelled me into success after success more than I could ever have dreamed. And they were smart. They knew that when I did well, they did well.

Learn to ask the questions you want answers to. You do this by being clear, concise, certain, and confident without imagining you're being pushy, arrogant, or superior. This isn't you, so don't allow anyone to tell you differently, if they dare to give you feedback such as this. (We'll talk about feedback a little later.)

And if you're already in a role and have never done this before and now want to begin creating a relationship with your manager, do the above actions: ask for a meeting and let your manager know why you're meeting with her or him. This is strategy 2, which we will move on to once you've completed your powerful practice for this step.

❖ Powerful Practice—Strategy 1

There are two practices for this strategy.

1. Have a go at drafting a strategic plan for your career based on the three facets I talked about: career development, career progression, and your earnings capacity. Don't overthink it. If at this stage, it's just a visionary plan, write it. Use all the information you gathered together in P1.
2. Next, brainstorm the true questions you'd love to be able to ask at an interview. Go outside the norm and the stock standard questions. Imagine you've been told you can ask anything you want. What would those questions be?

CHAPTER 46

How to Ask; Strategy 2: Setting Expectations for Yourself and Your Manager

In order to for you and your manager to work together well and have clarity about your working relationship, I believe setting expectations for you both is essential. Previously we talked about teaching people how to treat you. This is the professional application of that principle.

A key aspect of this strategy? You have to be the one following up not only on what you said you'd do but what your manager said he or she would do too.

Usually when I say this there's a sharp intake of breath and a nervous question. "I have to follow up with my manager?"

Yes, you do. Before we get to how you do this, let's talk about setting expectations that move you and your manager forward in delivering what the organisation needs, to the satisfaction of all concerned.

Relationships between managers and employees can be heavenly or hellish. Statistics state most employees leave their employment because of their managers. I believe this is a tragedy that underlines that we are still falling short of educating and coaching our managers to be leaders. Having been a manager for more than fifteen years in the corporate world, managing a team of one to almost forty, I learned how to be a manager and leader from my managers (the good ones), plus some amazing education along the way, and it's been one of the highlights of my career.

There are a number of factors to building a highly successful relationship with your manager to the extent you can set expectations and follow up without feeling like you've become a schoolteacher.

❖ First, remember that your manager is a human being (even if he or she doesn't give that impression) who wants to succeed, be outstanding in what he or she does, and make a difference in the work. Just like you.

❖ Next, as you're thinking about sitting down with them either for your first meeting in a new job, or a first meeting in a current role (because you haven't sat down with them before, or in a long while), think about how what you do in your role truly feeds into what they do, and how you can help them do it better in the short, medium, and long term.

○ The aim here is to brainstorm ways of helping to make their lives (and yours in the long run) easier as you plan your strategic career journey in this role (with an eye to the next milestone).

❖ Third, once you've had some thoughts about these, ask your manager to book in a time to meet with you, briefly letting him or her know why, and *you* book the meeting in the manager's diary, sending any material as you see fit.

❖ In the meeting, begin by sharing the information below, ensuring your language is always inclusive and collaborative, and at the end, simply ask if this is agreeable. Not whether it's okay (you're not asking for permission), you're just checking in to see if there's anything to add? Share:

○ why you requested the meeting;

○ what you'd like to discuss; and

○ the outcomes for both you hope to walk away with.

❖ In this first meeting, the kinds of topics you might want to discuss could include

○ shared goals—yours and theirs;

- their views on these shared goals in depth (they may have strong views on how they work etc. you want to know this);
- how you work best (educate them on how you like to work and be managed);
- what you're hoping to achieve in alignment to their goals (opportunity to check in and see if they agree);
- discussion on how you two will work together—this is critical, and you must discuss and agree how you will work together to deliver on the shared goals, because you see this as a team effort;
- how often you'd like to meet with him or her[1]; and
- how you will both follow up with each other in your meetings.

❖ Thank the manager for the meeting and his or her time, let the person know you'll be booking in the next meeting, and make sure you follow up and through.

By talking openly in this way at the first meeting, you get a feel for your manager and the manager for you. In the next meeting you can make any changes as you see fit for it to be better. If your manager likes short, sharp meetings, keep them short and sharp. Adapt to this person, ensuring it also works for you. At the end of the day this is a two-way relationship, and your ability to speak up and articulate what is important to you is vital in being productive *and* fulfilled.

Your ability to set and manage expectations—of what you will do and what your manager has agreed he or she will do—and then follow up on them, lets the other party know you take full ownership and accountability for yourself (principle 1 from chapter 39) and for asking where they are. In this you must be brave, dignified, and respectful.

---

[1] This is the clincher. I highly recommend this be the one objective of this meeting you must achieve, because the more you meet with and talk to your manager, the more opportunity you'll have to build a relationship, and most importantly, talk about what you've accomplished and how you intend to deliver the remainder of your goals.

You both have a vested interest in the success of the other, and it feeds into the art of creating true win-win solutions that are coming soon!

❖ **Powerful Practice—Strategy 2**

This is a simple one.

1. Put a date in the diary once you're ready (don't wait too long after you finish this book) to have the expectations conversation with your manager. Put it in your diary and then book it into your manager's!

CHAPTER 47

How to Ask; Strategy 3: Building the Relationship; Getting to Know Your Manager inside and Out

The first time I ever talked about this topic, I remember a vehement protest from a lady in the audience who came to speak to me after I'd finished addressing the group. She told me in no uncertain terms that the last thing she ever wanted was to get to know her manager.

This is certainly understandable, and I'm not asking you to become their best friend. Far from it. One of the challenges of management and leadership can be of creating boundaries, if you have developed solid friendships between managers and employees, which was the case for me. It can be done, but this is not what I want to talk about here.

I'd like to discuss the notion that if there's one person in your career who can help or hinder you the most, it's your manager. This is why in the previous step we talked about setting expectations to ensure there is a relationship that works for both of you. When it doesn't, it can be very painful, which is why we must start as we mean to go on, so we can know the truth sooner rather than later.

In order for you to be able to create true win-win scenarios for you and your manager, and ultimately your organisation, which is the next step, you're going to need to know what makes your manager tick, and the way to do this is by getting to know him or her.

I consider myself to have been very blessed with almost all the people I was managed by. I got to know them at a professional and personal level, and in doing this, I was able to do the one thing all managers hope and pray for—try to make their lives a little easier! I didn't always succeed, but I know I always gave it my best shot. They mattered to me.

Getting to know your manager is a far easier concept than you imagine, and because you're doing it with the intention of helping both of you be more successful, the strategy we utilise is "the power of questions." The easiest way of getting to know someone is to ask powerful questions in order to elicit the answers you need to create true win-win situations.

Once you start meeting with your manager on a regular basis, one of the things you always want to do (other than follow up) is have a list of questions for each meeting, whereby you can get additional information to help you fine-tune all the work you're doing.

Outstanding managers are a mine of information. They have access to people, resources, and knowledge, which you'll need in order to be better so they can deliver better too. When you ask the kinds of questions that will give you the insights you need, your career and work begin to have a strategic slant, and a savvy manager will notice this.

What are the questions you want to ask? You might want to know:

❖ What's important to them in their role?
❖ What are their goals? (And how do they tie in to your own?)
❖ What keeps them up at night? (You might have to find a diplomatic way of asking this one!)
❖ Do they have information about your area, the business, or the organisation as a whole they can share with you?
❖ How is the business doing?
❖ What are their and the organisation's strategic priorities?
❖ What challenges do they face?
❖ And most importantly, how can you assist them?

These are a sample of the questions you can ask, and in asking them and gaining the information you need, you continue to improve.

If you have a manager who isn't very forthcoming or one who simply isn't keen on sharing— sadly, there are managers who are insecure and believe the more they know and the less you do, the more successful they are—get creative in the way you structure your conversations with him or her. If the manager is reluctant to meet with you on a regular basis, try to catch up when you can, and be prepared when you do. Ensure the intent of your conversations are always transparent (as we talked about in chapter 38), and always phrase this intent in how it is a win for them. This could be through understanding what is important to them and articulating this, or in sharing how what you are doing is going to be a win for them (as well as you), the team and the organisation.

Sometimes you will come across managers who hinder you on your journey, either consciously or subconsciously. There is no simple or clever answer to this. You have to make a decision as to how hindered you are and whether a move into another role within the same organisation or a new one might be an option. Sometimes you can provide feedback to your manager's manager if things become really serious, but this is a whole topic in and of itself, and one that exceeds the scope of this book.

Do what you must from a place of transparency and pure intention for both of you, and communicate it as such in the hope you have one of the good ones, or if you're like me, many of the outstanding ones.

With the the information you learn from them, keep adding to your plan, keep sharing your wins with them, and keep asking the questions. This is how we get the answers we need!

❖ Powerful Practice—Strategy 3

1. Brainstorm questions you can ask your manager in all your meetings based on what is shared in each one and your assimilation and application of it, and then keep going!

CHAPTER 48

How to Ask; Strategy 4: Creating Powerful Win-Win Situations through Collaborations

This strategy builds on what we've talked about so far, concerning how once you have started building your relationship with your manager by getting to know them, continuing to set expectations, following up, assmimiliating, and applying to your plan the information you receive from them, it's time to become even more strategic: start thinking bigger and understand the broader sphere we are part of.

The concept of win-win isn't a new one, but it's rare that I've come across scenarios where both parties truly embrace this notion and live it. We still seem to live in a world where the model is one of scarcity (i.e. in order for me to win, you have to lose). I think this is balderdash, and I've lived the opposite, so I know that true and sincere win-wins really can happen.

I choose to live the belief and premise about people, as I shared with you earlier in chapter 40, that we are all one, so it would completely go against my principles to live anything other than this when it comes to my professional life. My experience of real win-wins across my career helped me get where I wanted to, and I believe I helped many people along the way get what they wanted too, as well as help the organisation move and evolve in the direction it was choosing.

This is the art of the true win-win, when through open, transparent communication, as you do your work, not only are you thinking about how you can succeed and be fulfilled; you're thinking about how what you're doing is a win for your manager and the organisation and how they can succeed and be fulfilled.

It's a win for your manager when the work you deliver to a very high standard aligns and feeds into their goals, thereby making their lives a bit easier, and the more you communicate and work together, the more you learn, the more you apply, the more it all grows.

Creating the win for the organisation is about stepping outside your role, your manager's role, and seeing the bigger picture. Understanding how you and the work you do feeds into the organisation, and then being creative about how to do it better, and most importantly, being commercial, i.e. understanding how the organisation makes *its* living (financially, operationally, reputationally etc.) in your approach, is key.

Commercial astuteness appears to be a skill lacking in many companies and organisations, and I've had many people say to me, "But my role isn't a commercial one." If you have a role within a business or any kind of organisation, be it also in the public or not-for-profit sector, it's commercial.

Businesses and organisations are usually in existence to make a profit or find a way to continue operating sustainably for the long term future in order to create that which they set out to do in the first place. Even not-for-profit organisations need to be commercial in a sense, otherwise they don't survive. Your role in whatever capacity you work in has been created to fulfil a need, and it fits into the model somehow. Therefore, your challenge is to create what is called a "line of sight" between what you do and what the organisations aims to achieve, and understand whether you help them save money (cost efficiency) or make money (revenue generating), or you could be doing both.

This is not a simple task, and it takes time, patience, and a willingness to think outside yourself far more than you can ever imagine. You have to map your role to the goals of the organisation and slowly understand all the moving parts and how they all tie together. It's not impossible—you just have to be prepared to take your time, learn it, and apply it.

Too many people diminish themselves and the role they occupy in the company they are in by playing it small. Not asking the questions they want to, or maybe don't realise they could, and working through their career, one thing after another without ever pausing and saying, "What are we (you, your manager, team, and the company) trying to achieve, and how do I fit into this so I can be and do better?"

When you begin demonstrating a commercial awareness and astuteness within your role, making your world bigger than it is, sharing this with your manager and possibly even broader, real magic can happen!

I learned to be and do this by having amazing managers who I observed and determined I would learn from. I started asking questions, stepping outside my space, learning more and more, and the more I developed and grew, the more my career developed and progressed, and I started receiving the money I wanted. I was also getting promoted and receiving and creating new opportunities faster than I dreamed possible. This is the magic that is available to all of us!

Understanding your industry and field as discussed in P1 is not only so you can ask for more money, it's about doing meaningful, passionate, evolving work throughout your career, helping you and everyone around you grow and succeed.

And the third part of this step—whenever you're talking about win-win scenarios, always talk as much as possible about how much of a win it is for them and all the ways it's a win for them, first and foremost.

The old adage of "What's in it for me?" is always a good axiom to follow when thinking about how wins are constructed. Step into the shoes of your manager, the other, the CEO if that's what you aspire to. Understand the whole picture, its component parts, and how it can be better, and you are on your way not only to six figures but high six figures!

❖ Powerful Practice—Strategy 4

1. In the role you are now in, have a go at doing what I have suggested above. Try to go as far out from yourself to the organisation as you can and you'll see how big the big picture really is. Go on, give it a go!

215

CHAPTER 49

How to Ask; Strategy 5: Seeding the Conversations and Testing the Water

We're now heading into P2, practice, and P3, which is the art of being the consummate professional.

P2 is a relatively short segment because it's simply about the art of practising the techniques we will talk about. As much as you can, practice with people outside your workplace or even with a coach like me. How powerful do you imagine it is when you start practising with your manager?

I mean, it makes sense. This is the person you'll be talking to and making the request of, so why not practise with him or her? Of course, I don't mean practise the actual "asking" conversation, but how about laying more foundations with them, so when you do ask, it's not a shock to either of you?

This is where strategy 5 comes in.

Now that you've been talking to your manager on a regular basis—monthly is a good frequency, I find—you no doubt feel much more confident about where you are in relation to the deliverables you have in your role, and your career as a whole.

In these conversations, as you talk about career development, it makes sense to share with your manager in subtle ways how the path of your career development feeds into your career progression and your earning capacity and potential (i.e. what you're aspiring to receive). This is where your intelligence into remuneration in your field and industry, if continuously and consistently kept abreast of, can reap you many rewards!

This is also where far too many women have either ended the conversation or never even had the conversation in the first place about the money they want. It can become a place where you can end up with promotions and not necessarily raises. Too many women in my experience have been too eager to say yes to the extra responsibilities their manager has offered them and yet, have either not taken the time to ask to be able to go away and reflect what this means for their current rate of remuneration (extra responsibility doesn't always mean a raise), if the extra responsibility is a significant addition to their role, what that extra work may equate to from a dollar/pound perspective.

This is where, as you communicate with your manager and share your progress, you ensure you share your development, and if your manager or company hasn't provided clear guidelines on how to progress in the organisation, once again you start asking subtle questions as to what that might look like, what your manager's expectations would be for you to achieve this, and if appropriate, talk about timelines and milestones.

Again, ask the questions you need answers to—and to help you make sure you don't sound like a broken record, says social media expert Gary Vaynerchuck, who wrote the book *Jab, Jab, Jab, Right Hook*, space out your questions about progression and potential raises in the timeline of your meetings. What I mean by this, and what Gary talks about is you give, give, and give, now you ask.

In the scope of your meetings, ask once a quarter about your progression and potential pay raises based on your development and progression. If your organisation has clear policies, take these into account before asking your questions, and as a matter of guidance, you ideally don't want to be talking about a raise within the first six months of a role, unless a truly unique occurrence has happened.

Manage yourself and your development, progression, and earning capacity as a medium- and long-term strategy, never short-term. Keep your plan up to date, and seed the conversations regularly to ensure you are building the confidence you need to be able to have the actual "asking" conversation.

This is the strategy of seeding, to give you the opportunity to practice talking about money in the context of your career development, progression, and the deliverables you are delivering.

Money is a deeply emotive subject—no one really likes talking about it, even the people who are good at asking. However, for you to get comfortable about asking, by using the strategy of seeding, you give yourself permission to practice and gain comfort, certainty, and confidence for when you do have the conversation.

This is one strategy I would encourage you to maximise as much as possible!

We're also going to talk in this chapter, about how you can bring up the initial enquiry into a potential pay raise, promotion, or opportunity. This doesn't mean we're going to ask outright. It means we're going to ask about asking. We're testing the water.

This helps you to start getting over the fear, because I know, even after all the work you've done, there will be some fear, and this is normal. We don't want to lose our fear (you remember what it really is, don't you – *False Evidence Appearing Real*) as we don't want to become complacent.

So, we're going to ask about asking.

Asking for anything, for a woman, is the one of the hardest thing to do—not only in our professional lives but in our personal lives. There are many reasons we don't ask, and there has been in-depth research into why women don't ask for raises. If you're interested in this, Linda Babcock and Sara Laschever are are excellent writers on this topic.

The reasons we don't ask range from not being groomed to ask from a young age, settling for less and thinking we're doing well, to learning to ask for less to ensure we don't appear to be pushy—too many reasons and one outcome. We have a pay gap between what women and men receive for work done, and for doing the same/similar work at a global level.

Therefore, in this strategy, you're going to select an appropriate meeting in your timeline, considering any salary-review timelines your organisation already has, and you're going to ask your manager some simple questions about what his or her thoughts are on how you're developing, what he or she sees as your progression, and what his or her views are on promotions.

This is a fact-finding mission and a practise session, which means you must ask the questions with the intention of letting your manager know this topic is of deep interest to you and an integral part of your career plans.

When you approach this conversation using all three concepts at once—development, progression, and earning capacity—it makes it easier to flow the conversation into the money aspect. Talk about your development and delivery, how you intend to progress as a part of your career and as it stands now, and how and what kinds of earning potential could these create for you?

Flow the conversation from one to the other, and it won't seem as nerve-racking. Give it a go!

❖ Powerful Practice—Strategy 5

Two practices for this strategy.

1. Thinking about strategy 5, what would be some of the work you could do in preparation for the seed meetings you will have with your manager once a quarter, and how will you ensure you maintain and retain your equilibrium?

2. Next, think about the kinds of questions you can ask as above, write them down, and if you prefer, practise them with a friend or coach. How do you come across? Does your voice tremble when you get to the money part? Ask for feedback from your practising partner and get comfortable and confident in this space. The big "ask" is almost here!

CHAPTER 50

How to Ask; Strategy 6: The Big Ask!

This is it—P3, where the rubber hits the road!

P3 is about being the consummate professional, irrespective of the outcome. For us to be and live the woman we are, we must choose to be the ultimate professional in every situation, especially when we have put ourselves on the line, asked for something, and potentially not received it. How we choose to be when things don't go our way is sometimes even more important than how we are when things do go our way.

This is the area that a lot of women are interested in, yet many women have confided in me they don't ask for raises, promotions, and opportunities, and they simply want to know how to. Given how much inner work you've already done, I'm hoping when you move through the next few sections of content, most of it won't seem as daunting, as it may have done before.

A lot of the information I share with you are general principles of remuneration and reward, based on my twenty plus years of being in the industry at an international level, but, as with all information, make sure you do as much research specific to your situation (I have shown you how in chapters 41 to 44), and ensure you're always adapting, tailoring, and being flexible in your approach. One size does not fit all.

There are several instances where you may be in a position to ask for a raise, promotion, or opportunity. This is by no means an exhaustive list, as doors open all the time, so keep your eyes and ears open. Many of my requests came from non-existent instances that I chose to pursue as a potential avenue of progression, and most of the time, they panned out. Instances can include:

- ❖ A new job offer with a new company;
- ❖ You've taken on, or are about to take on, more responsibility;
- ❖ You're ready for the next level/stage in your career;
- ❖ You believe you're underpaid, and you'd like to receive the remuneration you want;[2]
- ❖ You've identified an opportunity, and you're ready for it; and
- ❖ You've noticed an opening where nothing is in place, and you have an idea how you could add even more value and be rewarded for it.

Rather than any of the conversations above being a time of excitement and anticipation, for most women, it is fraught with tension, worry, and fear. If you find yourself falling into the group of women who become worried and panic, the questions to ask are: Why am I worried? What is it about this situation within me that is allowing me to feel this way?

Pinpoint the issue, deal with it (remember from step 1 where you identify what is triggering you and getting in your way and step 3, where if you need to go deeper, you know how to) and move forward. This stage is the whole reason for your journey at its core—even though there's been many other benefits—this is why you began this in the first place.

These kinds of questions are also perfectly normal when we go to do something we've never done before, or maybe have tried before and didn't succeed. It's okay to be scared and keep going.

There are also a couple of myths I'd like to debunk as we go through this section, in the hope you'll come to realise the world can tell you all it wants—it's your choice as to whether you believe it—or you can simply test the notion for yourself and make up your own mind.

Growing up as a feisty, opinionated little Indian girl (not much has changed), I learned early on that for me to be able to live the life I chose,

---

[2] Your emotional state is integral in this scenario.

I would have to challenge the status quo. I did, and this taught me that nothing is true for me, unless I've experienced it for myself. Even then I kept going until what I chose was what I received. My father always did say I was a stubborn little scut!

So, myth one: Women have shared with me their concern that if they were to ask for a pay raise, promotion, or opportunity, or even bring up the subject; their manager or interviewer and the company might think they were greedy, grasping, and arrogant.

Answer: I think you know my views on this based on what I've shared previously, but let me immediately dissuade you of this notion once and for all.

Organisations must evolve to stay alive and be profitable, in whichever manner this may be for them; and when you view yourself and your career in the way we have been discussing, and you actively live this, any leader in a company worth anything will see this and be glad to have you on the team. If not, you, in your brilliance, will come to know and understand you must then find the environment where this will be true for you.

There's a more commercial slant to this discussion too. As you progress up the ladder within an organisation or even simply in your own career, you will be picking up more skills and experience, and you will be asked to become involved in higher-level responsibilities.

If you don't know how to negotiate for yourself, how do you suppose it looks when you may need to be in a position where you must negotiate, influence, and persuade as part of your job?

Many women have told me they are great at negotiating for others, just not so good for themselves, and I know this to be true, having seen it time and time again. The challenge with this is if you're discussing a new job or promotion and are unable to ask for yourself, as great a negotiator as you may be on behalf of the company, the person opposite hasn't yet had the opportunity to experience you in this way and may take your inability to negotiate for yourself as an example of this skill you say you possess but don't show.

I can't remember how many conversations I've had with managers and senior managers who, after an interview or meeting, have turned to me and told me, as much as they may have liked the woman in the room, her inability to ask for what she wanted made them doubt her ability to ask on behalf of the organisation. Don't do this to yourself. Don't lose out because you didn't ask, especially when you can!

The ability to ask for what you want is a critical skill, and one you might want to start practising at every available opportunity. The more you practise and get to know about what you are doing, the better equipped and confident you'll feel, and then it becomes a pleasure, not a chore.

Myth 2: Many women tell me they don't ask for raises, promotions, and opportunities because they think if the company had the money to pay them extra, or give them the promotion or opportunity, they would have done so. The other aspect of this is, "I work really hard and I do a great job, so they should just give me the raise and promotion."

Sometimes this works and many times it doesn't. Why? Let me address the second part first.

Managers are busy people, and they may think you're amazing, and when the time is right, they will put you forward. In the meantime, they may have whole teams, projects, and responsibilities to manage, as well as excel in themselves, so they too can be promoted. If you're not sharing with your manager how well you're going, seeding conversations and then asking (i.e. taking responsibility and ownership for your career and earning capacity), then what's the likelihood they will do this for you?

Not to be unkind, but highly unlikely!

First, the likelihood their career is at the forefront of their mind, and second, they may have a very high performing team, so why would you stand out? This is why you *must* take ownership of the conversations and your career.

Now, to the first part of myth two, the idea that if a company has the money, they should simply pay you.

The first time I heard this, given I worked in remuneration, it surprised me because I'd mistakenly assumed everyone understood how salary budgets worked. In many of my roles as head of reward, I'd do my best to educate my employee populations on how remuneration works, but I realised it doesn't always stick.

The biggest barrier to asking for a raise is something I mentioned earlier—the organisation's ability and choice to pay and their remuneration policies, and this is where your commercial astuteness comes into play.

If an organisation is facing cash flow issues (big or small), one of the first areas to be frozen is pay. This is because often, the biggest cost for many companies is labour, therefore if times are hard, this is the first area where efficiencies will be sought. Hence the abundance of redundancies and restructuring we've been seeing in the last few years. Companies are seeking to find more and more ways of getting more done through less resources, or the utilisation of more technologies, and this is a challenge for all concerned, especially the people in the company. No one likes letting people go.

This is not to say an organisation won't pay if it needs to. If you've demonstrated how you add significant value and they want to retain you, the likelihood is the raise requested is a better financial option than potentially having to re-recruit, retrain, wait for someone to join and then settle in if you chose to go elsewhere. Become highly familiar with the way your organisation operates financially, and you'll have an edge on how this thinking process works.

The other thing to remember is sometimes the organisation may have the money, but if paying you extra throws some of their pay practices out of alignment, they may decline to pay you extra. They may decide instead to offer you another package item, a non-monetary reward. This doesn't happen very often if the candidate is valued at what is being asked, and if they need him or her, so make sure you are prepared and can be the exception.

A lot of companies do take their pay practices seriously, and many don't want anomalies, as this can create problems down the line, so simply be aware of this as a factor in your asking process.

Sometimes the money just won't be there. If that's the case, you're either going to have to bide your time until times get better or look for another job.

Now that the two biggest myths have been dispelled, let's get into the nuts and bolts of the "asking conversation."

The main theme of P3 is about taking all of P1 and P2, the preparation and practice, and getting ready for having the "asking conversation." The intention of that conversation, based on all our work, must be, "Who and how will I be?"

CHAPTER 51

How to Ask; Strategy 7: The Asking Conversation

I've constructed P1–3 as a three-stage process, and we will go through each stage to ensure crystal-clear clarity for you as you apply it in your own life. You will have noticed I like doing things step by step, and I hope this is supporting you as you build your plan. As I said earlier, there's nothing worse than getting to a point where you don't know what to do next.

This is a lengthy chapter, so take your time in digesting what you learn here, and then break it down as appropriate for you, based on your requirements.

The three stages of the conversation are:

- ❖ Stage 1—prior to the conversation;
- ❖ Stage 2—during the conversation; and
- ❖ Stage 3—post-conversation

Stage 1—Putting yourself in the space, prior to the conversation

Getting to the stage of being able to have the conversation simply requires taking all you have learned so far and applying it in a systematic fashion. To help you summarise your preparation, below are some powerful questions and principles to assist you.

❖ Why am I having this conversation? Is my intention aligned to my overall purpose and career aspirations, as well as being true to myself?

❖ Get your agenda out of the way. Having the conversation is not a time to grind an axe or compare yourself to anyone else. It's about communicating the value that you add and asking for the salary this equates to.

❖ It is not about your worth—it's about the financial compensation you receive for the job you do and the significant value you add in what you do for all concerned.

❖ Detachment to the outcome—regardless of what happens, who you are and what you are being and doing and your self-worth is always, in all ways intact before and after the conversation.

❖ Be clear on the potential outcomes. There are truly only two definitive outcomes to the conversation—yes and no. Remember, no is not always no!

❖ Always think win-win no matter what the potential outcomes, and define as clearly and with as much detail what this means for all parties concerned.

❖ Think through all the consequences of your reactions—your reaction will be what your manager remembers.

❖ Have I made a compelling case? Review your business case[3] and make sure it's thorough.

I mentioned in the last chapter there are many scenarios where you can ask for what you want, but the two main scenarios are:

---

[3] It is possible to do more than what is asked of you in your role without going outside the scope of it. Simply think through the implications of your work to the next level, and in doing so demonstrate, as we talked about earlier, your understanding of line of sight of your role as to why the company hired you in the first place. Operating this way in your career, utilising your strategic plan in the areas of development, progression, and growing your earning capacity means you're always growing and hopefully creating many references to support your business case.

❖ Asking for a raise when you're already in a role (can be applied for promotions and opportunities); and

❖ Asking in a new role in a new organisation.

To build a plan and business case, which we will discuss in detail, simply utilise the information below and adapt it to your particular scenario. The better you get at this, the stronger your requests will become.

Stage 2—Having the conversation
Already in a Role

With both scenarios, the key as always is preparation.

In most companies when a manager or interviewer either needs to recruit or give a pay increase, they must provide a business case, as to why they should be given that resource.

When thinking about asking for a raise, I'd highly recommend you take the same approach.

Most managers, when it comes to raises, especially ones they aren't initiating, are thinking, *why should I give you more money when you're doing the job I hired you to do? And I don't care if the market has moved— what makes you think you deserve a raise?*

This is not a manager being a jerk, simply a manager who handles a budget with a limited amount of money allocated for people activity, and who may also have to go further up the chain to justify a raise. This may likely be the case if your request is not part of an annual review process and may be outside the remuneration policy of the organisation. As you can see, there are several moving parts for you manager to work through too!

Therefore, if you have an appreciation of what your manager is ruminating on, use this to your advantage for the benefit of yourself and the organisation. Remember, always think win-win, with the intention of articulating the win for them first.

One of the best and simplest ways of asking for a raise when you're already in a role is:

❖ By documenting all your successes, achievements, and accomplishments throughout the role, including:

- ○ the money you have saved the company;
- ○ the efficiencies you have created;
- ○ the work you have done further to what was asked of you in your role, but not outside the scope of it;
- ○ the initiative you have shown; and
- ○ what you will continue to be and do to add significant value.

However, stay within the scope of your role, because if you go outside it and do the work without it being an agreed inclusion of responsibility, it could mean you've just lost out on the additional remuneration due to you.

I've seen many women do this to their own detriment. I did it early in my career, only to realise being in remuneration that often the extra responsibility warranted a raise—for example, the job got bigger—and I, in my naiveté, did two things: one, not ask for the extra remuneration, and two, assumed it would be given to me.

If your role becomes bigger, you need to at least find out whether the additional responsibilities warrant additional compensation. You also need to ask for it there and then, not three months down the line. By then it's easier to say no, and you've taught them how to treat you.

Saying that, there is one truth no one likes hearing: no one is going to pay you extra for doing your job.

The time for such a mind-set is swiftly passing. Having worked in performance management and reward for twenty plus years, I can see how fast companies are moving into this space, where only the people who perform above a certain level are being rewarded with better than average raises and bonuses. This is due to the fact, as I mentioned before there are limited budgets—having to do more with less—to maintain and create better efficiency ratios within a business, and make sure only the people who are performing are being rewarded above the norm.

If you're not, or haven't been one of these people and you want to debate with me that you already work your knuckles to the bone and you're not being rewarded, then:

- ❖ You think you're one of those people, and your manager doesn't think you are;
- ❖ You are one of those people and your manager doesn't realise it (have you shown him or her?); and
- ❖ Your manager knows but still hasn't given you the raise you want. In which case, you can have another go with all you've learnt in this book, and if the answer is still no, then you can decide if you want to stay in the job or not. It's your choice.

How do you show your manager that you deserve a raise? If your organisation has a salary-review process, and although you're sure you'll get a raise, you want a bigger raise or promotion or opportunity, then you might consider doing the following as part of your strategy. I will also share with you how to time your additional raise a little later.

Create your own business case for the raise, ensuring you've done all the work as discussed prior to getting to this point. There may be overlaps, but you get the picture.

- ❖ Make sure throughout the year you are cataloguing all the work you are doing, documenting all your successes, accomplishments, and "failures," noting what didn't worked and what you learned from it and did differently the next time.
- ❖ Make sure you're meeting with your manager on a regular basis to inform him or her of what you are achieving.
- ❖ Ask your manager what more you can do to assist him or her, and then document it.
- ❖ Document anything you are asked to do outside your original remit, or if you're suddenly asked to do work that was not on your goals for the year.
- ❖ Document everything, and be specific about your accomplishments.
- ❖ Try to allocate as much financial and non-financial measurements as you can of all your achievements.

❖ Only include data about the state of remuneration in the current market for your field if it is relevant. If the market has moved and you know you could be valued at a higher level, include this. Otherwise leave it alone.

Anyone who approaches a manager with a solid business case will:

❖ Let the manager see your ability in documenting and presenting such a case. It doesn't have to be *War and Peace*. Quality always beats quantity.
❖ Help their manager remember the skills and initiative you have shown in doing this.
❖ Help them make a considered decision, and if needed, utilise the business case for the next level of sign off as required.

In a pay-increase conversation with your manager, the best way of managing this conversation is to be clear, concise, and calm. Remember, your manager already knows you!

Talk your manager through your business case. Make sure you highlight all the areas where you have added value, used your initiative, and exceeded expectations. Answer any questions they may have. Explain your request clearly and calmly, and listen to what they say.

Communicate everything thoroughly and make sure you have a written copy of your business case they can take away with them, if they need to review it.

If, after you've finished sharing your business case, your manager either says no right away or after a pause, first take a deep breath. Remember who you are, stay calm no matter what is going on inside you, and ask for a reason. Is there a lack of budget? An inability at this present time to action the raise for another reason? Find out the real reason, and here's the key—don't be brushed off.

You have every right to ask the question and expect a reasonable answer. Simply make sure you stay calm and reasonable. Maintain your composure and on no occasion, should you threaten to resign, especially if you have no intention of following through. You will lose too much credibility if you say you will resign and then you don't.

I would recommend not saying someone else will give you what you're asking for, unless you have an actual job offer, as a manager may ask you to demonstrate it. You don't have to, but of course, it goes back to your credibility; so, don't say it if you can't back it up. I've experienced too many conversations like these where people think it won't be followed up. It is.

If the outcome is no and your manager has explained to you thoroughly why this is the case, make sure you thank your manager for his or her time, go away, and think about it. Don't make any rash decisions, and I will share with you how best to deal with no a little later.

Being who you choose to be, I know you'll want to maintain your credibility and integrity throughout this process, as it will stand you in a strong and powerful place for the future, in your career and in your ability to always be able to ask for what you want. Therefore, be the powerful woman you are throughout.

Below are some summary pointers for having this conversation with your manager.

❖ Feel good—you are taking action and having the conversation.
❖ Thank your manager for his or her time.
❖ Explain why you asked for the meeting.
❖ Summarise your request.
❖ Pull out your business case—make sure you have two copies so you can both reference it in the meeting.
❖ Take them through the business case.
❖ Pause—let the information digest.
❖ Answer any questions honestly and candidly.
❖ Pay attention to body language and gauge what they may want to know additionally.
❖ Ask for thoughts—do they have any additional questions?
❖ Remember, if your manager has to get additional sign off (assume this to be the case), you want your manager's buy-in at

this stage. Make sure he or she has a copy of the business case and provide any further copies if needed.

Offer in a New Role

A lot of what I have mentioned above will apply; however, with a new role, there is less emotion involved, as you haven't yet started there and you're not too concerned with how other people might regard you (in the nicest way possible)—just yet.

The key with this scenario too is preparation.

Although you will have done your research about remuneration in your field and industry, one thing to remember is that within your field, depending on which industry you go into, the salary may vary. Make sure you have an idea of what your role is valued at in the industry you have applied for.

Stack the odds in your favour by being very clear about what level of remuneration is acceptable to you. You've got through the interview process, so clearly, they want you—now you must just make sure the money matches the role.

Since you know what the remuneration level is, the next thing to remind yourself about is where you are in relation to that level, with the skills and experience you have. Most remuneration is likely to be categorised into:

- ❖ Minimum
- ❖ Median
- ❖ Maximum

Remuneration surveys may talk in quartiles or percentiles—25th, 50th, 62.5th, 75th, 90th, etc.

If your skills, experience, and accomplishments (based on all those job mappings you did previously) match at the higher level, then aim your expectation from the 50th percentile to the 75th, or from the median to the maximum. There is a drawback with positioning yourself here, and it is that within organisations where position to market is used as part of the salary review process, if you are a high performer and in the upper median quartile or percentile, your actual increase may be reduced, so consider your position to the market already.

Someone who is low in the market and a high performer may be allocated a higher percentage increase to bring them up more to market level.

If your skills, experience, and accomplishments are not quite there yet, but on the way, aim at the 50th percentile or just above the median.

Otherwise, stay between the high minimum and median.

Most organisations aim for the median and position high performers between the median and the maximum with the intention of supporting them to get to the next level.

Never try to sell yourself at a level you have not reached. You will lose credibility, and credibility is the name of this game.

Once you know where you are in this stage in the interview and recruitment process, you will have been given an idea of what the company is willing to pay.

Now, if at any point, you've been told what the company's expectations are and yours are much higher, do not continue unless you've been given some assurance they may consider your level of remuneration expectation. Only proceed if your salary expectation and the company's are in line, because therein lies the space to ask for what you want.

Make sure you have considered everything for yourself in relation to the level of remuneration you are asking. Have you added in all your costs?

Once you have all the data around remuneration—the markets, your value in this role—then you're in the place to have the offer conversation when it's time.

In an interviewing situation, whether you have this conversation with the organisation directly or through a recruitment agent, once you have clarity around what you want, it's a simple case of conveying it.

If the company or recruitment agent comes to you with an offer and you wanted $10,000 more, first of all, think about how close this number is to the original one you were advised of. If it's the same and you still want the extra because you believe you deserve it and are worth it, then ask for it. However, before you do … pause for thirty seconds after the offer, and then respond.

This is not a trick, and I'm not asking you to pause in the hope the gap will drive the number higher, although it can do that. This is a moment allowing you to reflect, check in with yourself, and give yourself the space to solidify your core so that if you do decide you want to ask for more, you do it from a space of powerful core consciousness and confidence.

By taking this time, you acknowledge the offer, what it means to you, and what you've done to receive it. If it's less than what you want, still, take the time to do this. If it's more or what you asked for, truly receive it from a soul place. If you're going to ask for more, receive it and know you have more to ask.

Thirty seconds can be a long time, and if you're on the phone rather than in person, simply ask the person on the other end if you can have a minute. You're only going to take thirty seconds.

In the space of those thirty seconds, a number of things will happen. They may say "sure" and give you the time you want. They may jump straight in and ask you what you think. They may quote a higher number. Whatever happens, don't be surprised if they try to fill the gap, because as we all know …

People don't like gaps of silence.

However, take the time you need, and if you're asking for more, simply ask for what you want. Use the words that resonate with you. You might say something like, "I was thinking more along the lines of $110,000 plus a 10 percent bonus. I believe this is reasonable given my skills and experience and the value I know I can add."

Wait for a response. Have the conversation you want to have from the place of you owning your worth, and ask for what you want. It is simply a conversation, a dialogue where you get to ask for what you want.

If you're talking to a recruitment agent, this could mean another call. That's okay. Be honest, but don't start playing hardball. Continue to be polite, and do the dance of asking.

If your request is reasonable and the company can pay it—remember they genuinely may not be able to—then it's likely you will get what you asked for. If not, at some point in the conversation, either the company or recruitment agent will come back and say, "This is the best they can do."

If their best is in your vicinity and you want the job, take it. If not, then it's your decision. Simply remember it's not always about asking for the sake of asking. We never ask without purpose. There may be a genuine reason they can't give you what you want right now.

Decide what you want, come from a place of abundance, and make your decision.

CHAPTER 52

How to Ask; Strategy 8: Key Tips to Asking

In whichever manner you decide to move in relation to asking for what you want, make sure you are totally comfortable with it. This will give you the confidence and certainty to push ahead, regardless.

Remember, this is not just about you—you want your manager and new employer to be impressed with your asking skills, and you want to ensure the atmosphere is all about win-win. As well as that, in a new role, it's likely the person you're asking this of may be your new manager—make sure he or she feels as good about the process as you do.

Think through all the responses the manager and/or new employer might come back with. Have all your data with you whether you end up having the conversation in an office or over the phone.

Don't get flustered or take it too seriously—remember, you're honing a skill, and this is not life or death. Practice really does make perfect.

You can also ask about other items of interest to you including professional growth and what your manager or new employer can offer you—development, career advancement opportunities, and other non-monetary rewards. Find out what is on offer, and make sure what you ask for is in alignment to that. It's not always about the money, however, given that we as women struggle in asking for the money, please make sure you're not telling yourself it's not about the money when it clearly is!

You also don't want to go in with an either/or mind-set. Ask for all that you'd like. Too many women settle, and you are worth all you choose to ask for, and the organisation will vastly benefit from you being a part of it.

Now to some key tips to asking.

Timing

One aspect of asking for what you want is in reference to the timing of your request.

In a current role, once you've taken into account any policies and processes your organisation already has, manage your asking within this scope. Things to bear in mind with this include

❖ The annual salary review process is not the best time to ask for an above average raise.
   ○ The reason is that the whole organisation has been allocated a budget for all employee raises, and each manager must manage a budget. For your manager to give you, for example, a 10 percent raise, he or she would have to take it from someone else's allocation, and often the manager is not willing to. Therefore, if your organisation has an annual review process, manage the whole of your pay raise request in context to this to get the best you can through the process, and then ask for the rest at a later point.
   ○ If the organisation also has a system that allocates percentage increases based on your performance rating and position to market, again for your manager to give you more, he or she has to take it from someone else and again the likelihood is he or she may not choose to.
   ○ Therefore, ensure you receive the best pay raise you can at this time, bearing in mind the constraints of the process.

❖ It's usually not a good idea to ask for a large raise within three months of a salary-review process. The likely answer will be, "You've just had a raise."

❖ The best time to ask for a raise is within a few months of a new financial year or budgets being set or when the raise, promotion, or opportunity is being funded by money you have saved your manager or created for him or her.

Many of my most successful requests came from identifying an opportunity where I could save my manager money or assist him or her in not having to spend extra to have something done, thereby earmarking those funds instead for me!

This could be in the form of someone leaving, and you realising that rather than your manager having to go through the whole recruitment process, you're able to absorb the responsibilities of that role. This allows you to request a reasonable increase to compensate you for your new, larger role and still saves your manager the remainder of the salary the new person would have received.

This is just one way you can create an opportunity out of thin air, but be mindful that you can succeed in what you have suggested. Don't set yourself up to fail!

In an interview for a new role, most employers will either have advertised or will mention remuneration at the very first interview; so, if your expectation is not in line with theirs and there is a big difference, don't waste your time or theirs. However, if they've told you the expectation and it's in the vicinity of what you're looking for and you've progressed through the interview phases—the further into the process you go, the stronger your position is.

As you progress, not every candidate that started out where you will have, so if you get to the final stage, it's likely there maybe you and one other candidate. Maybe two. This is a strong position to be in, even if there are other people.

Some interviewers will try to wrangle you into early conversations around remuneration—don't be drawn into it. You want to wait until you know you have a better-than-average chance toward the final-stage interview, when they must decide. The later in the process you are, the more likely an offer will be made, and the more likely an asking opportunity will arise for you.

To finish off this chapter, some final conversation pointers about asking:

❖ Maintain emotional confidence—who you are is critical to your success in this conversation, regardless of what the outcome may be.

❖ Be respectful of your manager (even if you had issues in the past).

❖ Don't be afraid to ask for an answer. If your manager is being noncommittal, explain respectfully that you'd appreciate a direct response, so that way you know where you stand.

❖ Get a directional answer if a firm one is not available to you right now.

  ○ Sometimes you'll get what you want, because the other party can let you have it.

  ○ Other times you might not, because there is a genuine reason why they can't give you the extra dollars.

❖ Don't despair or get huffy. Ask to be reviewed in six or twelve months, or ask for something else.

❖ Don't take it to a point that it becomes a battle of wills, because then not only have you lost the plot, you're likely to be antagonising the one person who can give you what you're asking for!

❖ Remember, the result for both parties always has to be a true win-win result and always lead with the win for them first!

CHAPTER 53

How to Ask; Strategy 9: The Outcome—Yes/No, and How to Deal with It

The potential outcomes of our asking conversation are

- ❖ yes: you got what you asked for—fantastic! or
- ❖ no: you didn't get what you asked for.

Please don't become dejected, say, "This doesn't work," or give up in any way. There are many reasons why it may be no, and we've talked about them in earlier chapters. If your manager says no, simply do the following, especially if it's said in the initial conversation.

Calmly and professionally ask why the answer was no. Give them the chance to articulate fully why the answer is no. Keep asking for reasons that make sense and are in alignment to what you know. If they must get additional sign off, this is not a no. Too many women hear this as a no and don't follow up.

In this case make sure you give them exactly what they need and make sure you continue to follow through. The only way this can peter out is if you let it go. Keep following through until you get a response.

If the reasons you're hearing no aren't resonating with you; you feel like you're being brushed off, stay in your centre and be transparent. Share with them a final time why you've asked, and if in spite all your requests and conversations the answer is still no, be the consummate professional. Close the meeting out by thanking them for their time and consideration, acknowledge your appreciation, leave them with a good taste in their mouth of the whole conversation, and let them know you'll be considering your options. A great phrase I have used and one I share with my clients that they love is, "Thank you very much for your time. I appreciate the conversations we had, and of course I am disappointed with this outcome. However, it's also a good reminder for me to consider my options." Or words to that effect.

This is a *not* a threat to resign. This is you—a powerful woman who knows she has options—choosing to reflect on those options and decide.

If you've decided it's time to move on, take the time to make sure this is your choice and not just a knee-jerk reaction to the conversation. Review and reflect on your choices, begin your search for your next opportunity, and maintain your excellence in all you're still doing in your current role. Remember, you'll likely need their reference, so never burn your bridges.

If you've decided to stay, again take the time and reflect, and then be brave and open the conversation with the utmost transparency with your manager as to what is next for you. Share your aspirations and keep moving forward with your plan.

Whatever you deem are your options, utilise them and remember this.

You remain in the driver's seat—why?

You, at your core, understand that each moment gives us a choice and all this is simply another moment of choice for you to decide who and what you will be. You are the owner of your career, and you decide what this will look like, knowing all your employers are simply co-collaborators adding value to each other as we do the dance of our careers.

For the remainder of this chapter we will complete P3, stage 3 of the "asking conversation."

Stage 3—Staying in the Space Post-Conversation

This is where who you are and who you are choosing to be is the most critical. Once you've had the conversation, life goes on, and you get to choose how you are going to continue to be. So now you have what you wanted, or not—what next?

Got What You Asked for: Now What?

Now you have the money or promotion or opportunity you wanted, what next?

I wanted to add this chapter because sometimes, once we get what we wanted, we can begin to take it for granted.

Nowadays, tenure in a role has fallen dramatically to what it used to be. People stayed in companies in the past for years and years. This is no longer the case. People will move on if they aren't getting what they need. Maybe in tough times people stayed; however, this isn't something we can rely on anymore. If you don't want to go, sometimes it's not even your choice.

So, what are the next few sections about?

They're about the guidance I'd like to give you to help you stay motivated and optimistic about the future—a future you create, because you are the creator of your career and life.

Regardless of what is happening in the world, we have control over the most important things in the world—our perceptions, attitudes, and responses.

Keep yourself in control of yourself, how you perceive what is happening around you, and how you respond to that, and you can rule the world. Put yourself in a place of faith and knowing; don't allow the outside world to tell you who you are and what you can achieve. You will achieve it and people will ask, "How do you do it?"

Well, now you know.

To continue being able to grow and receive more, if this is what you want, you must continue to excel and create outstanding results for yourself and your organisations, and you can do this by following the principles below.

Seek to Add Significant Value in Everything You Do

In everything you do relating to your job, look to add significant value. Ask yourself regularly, "How can I do this better than it has ever been done before?"

This is not about reinventing the wheel, discovering the cure for cancer, or anything like that. It becomes about excelling, growing—your focus widens, you take in more, you have better ideas and implementation—and before you know it, you're automatically thinking, *how can I be and do this better'* And when you get to this stage and start producing results, your results will speak for themselves.

Rather than just doing a task, think about why the task needs to be done, and then think of all the implications there are about getting that task done. The minute you start looking at the bigger picture, the big picture will start to include you, and adding significant value will become as natural to you as breathing. Recognition, reward, and opportunity automatically gravitate toward people who add significant value. Make sure you're one of them.

Build Relationships

I could talk about this subject forever, it's such a passion of mine! If you'll recall from the section on feminine and masculine energy—relationships, our ability as feminine women to be able to relate to all of life—is a core element of what fulfils us, and it is, from my experience and the experience of some outstanding leaders, one of the keys to real leadership.

By simply living from this space in a way that brings out the best in you and others, you will be ahead of the crowd. When you work in an organisation, you work with other people. Working with other people means being able to communicate, collaborate, and build solid win-win relationships with them.

The minute you enter a role, whether it's a new role with a new company, or a new role in another department, you need to find out who your stakeholders are and give them a stake in you and vice versa. Once they have a stake in you and you have one in them, without saying anything, it becomes a win-win relationship. My strategy for building this relationship?

Find out what your stakeholders need from you, and give it to them first.

And second.

And third.

And fourth …

You get the picture.

You're not doing this from some misguided notion of, "Maybe if I keep giving, they'll give me what I want." Hell no! You operate in this manner because you've worked through that when you give to them, you're also giving to you and to the organisation. Win-win!

You've worked through the strategy, your plan. You see how it all ties together, and you're smart in your execution, because you get it and you deliver it.

Outstanding!

Give Yourself Certainty

In life, we often find out very quickly that we can't control a lot of what is happening around us. Some of us realise this and become control freaks. Others become victims. Neither place is a great place to be, because we are at the mercy of uncontrollable factors. There is only one place you can be, and be happy.

And that is … to know you can only control yourself, and give yourself the certainty you need to be the powerful, creative woman you are.

In a new or even a current role, you will come across situations where you may find yourself thinking, *oh … what do I do now?*

Most of the time you can ask someone, get an answer, and find a way out. Sometimes you genuinely have to go elsewhere for advice. The key here is not to freak out.

There are always going to be times when you're not going to have the answer. Make yourself fine with that, and then remind yourself you may not have the answer to that, but you have answers to other things, and you have the capacity to find the answers you need.

In times of uncertainty, whether it's in your role, in the organisation, or in the industry, give yourself the certainty you seek. If you're asked to do something you've never done before and you're swimming in uncertainty, take a deep breath, calm down, and think about another time where you've had to face something you've never done before.

Think about how you solved that problem. Think of another time, and another, and another. Stack as many references as you need when in the face of an uncertain situation, and you will create confidence and certainty for yourself.

By simply being in that place—the answers will come. People or resources that can help you will turn up. They will. They always do. Have faith and trust; if you've found the answer before, you can do it again.

Remind yourself you are the only one who can give you certainty in an uncertain world, and you will never be at the mercy of someone else's whim.

Knock 'Em Dead!

Go into the role with the aim and intention of amazing them, wowing them, knocking 'em dead from surprise. Go into any venture with the strongest intention of knocking someone's socks off, so that person will say, "*Wow!*"

Don't go into a job wondering whether you will be able to succeed. Know that you will, and the reason you know that is because …

You are the secret to your success. You. No one else. You.

And because of that one, little fact, *you* will succeed.

Eye on the Horizon

We all know lives doesn't stand still.

For those of us who try to make life stand still, we can get knocked to the ground quickly, because we were standing still and life was moving on ahead of us. Don't get knocked down and wonder whether you will get up again or not.

You will.

It's a simple case of knowing that when you get knocked down, you get up. And you keep getting up, no matter how many times you get knocked down. Each time you do you will learn something new, and something better will come along.

Now the something better may be a while in coming, so you must trust the process and have faith it is coming. It's not always easy, but it is simple.

Wayne Dyer (God rest his soul) said, "Infinite patience produces immediate results. The immediate results infinite patience produces, is peace."

When you have peace in your core, in your soul, somehow, some way, you know you will find a way, or a way will be shown to you.

Seriously, trust and have faith. It will make sense.

Do Your Best, and Know You Always Have a Choice

If you have the soul, heart, mind, and body that you want to succeed, be and do all you can, and then leave the universe to bring you the fruits of your labour.

Sometimes we can be hammering at something we should have left alone a while ago, but because we're not trusting in the process, we're still trying to create results. Feel great, take inspired action, do your best to the extent of your abilities, and then let it go!

I firmly believe and have experienced many times in my life how the universe, God, energy—whatever you want to call it—has conspired with me to bring me the results I chose, often in ways I couldn't have imagined. Therefore, don't feel the need to flog a dead horse, and know one thing. No matter how bad things may get, you still have a choice.

You can decide to stay in a "bad" situation. You have the confidence and faith that this is going to get better, and if you believe it, then do it. If you decide not to stay, because you think you can do better elsewhere, then that's your choice too. Even when we have financial obligations and think we don't have a choice—we do.

Remember, by not deciding, we decide.

So, don't let anything or anyone or even your own beliefs and thoughts steal your power. You have a choice. You can make the decisions that are right for you and the people in your life, and no one has the power to say otherwise.

Grow, Don't Stagnate

Make the decision that no matter what, you will continue to grow.

Stretch yourself, keep learning, and don't go for the low-hanging fruit. It may be tasty, but you won't get as much satisfaction and joy as from knowing that you climbed the tree and got to the top. The more you grow, the more the universe rewards you. It might not always look the way you thought it would. Hindsight is a tremendous gift!

If you don't grow, you stagnate, and we all know what happens when things stagnate—they become obsolete and are usually thrown away, or they die.

Keep growing, and know that by being and doing this, not only will your dreams come true, you will become a leader and an example. In truth, you already are. Now's the time to live it.

CHAPTER 54

How to Ask; Strategy 10: Feedback Forever More!

One of the most critical aspects of making the decision to live in this way and manage your career and earning capacity strategically is, as part of the journey, you will need to ask for feedback.

Whether the answer is yes or no, you're going to want to receive feedback about the whole process and how the other person experienced the process too. If you're a manager, you're definitely going to want to know how the people reporting to you are experiencing you too.

Most people I know dislike feedback Dislike is probably putting it mildly. Similar to how most people dislike pay raise conversations, managers and employees have an aversion to asking for and receiving feedback, and the main reason is because we're terrible at giving meaningful feedback.

I don't claim to be an expert, but I know from my own experience of being a manager, a senior manager, and an employee there are ways to ask for and receive feedback in which both parties have a great experience.

I'm happy to share my experience, and if it serves you, I'm glad for it. If you'd like to learn more, there are many resources you could tap into. Find a way of doing this that works for you, and hone it.

My approach to feedback is something I shared earlier with you, about how I managed my teams. I knew as a manager and leader there would be times when I would have to deliver not-so-great news, and like everyone else, I hated it. However, I soon realised that, working in remuneration, I was going to have to learn how to have the tough conversations.

There are three principles I live by in this space: intention, openness, and responsibility.

Starting with intention, the key for me when it comes to giving and receiving feedback is that I always set expectations about this topic before I need to give feedback with any of my team or stakeholders, or now to my clients. I let them know early on in our relationship that if we're to ever have a feedback conversation, my intention will always be to help them to be and do better (the same for me), and therefore …

I am open to having as transparent a conversation as is required, and once I have shared my feedback, or if I am on the receiving end, after I receive it, then we will have an open discussion about all that was shared.

This then feeds into my third principle: in my openness, I will take responsibility for the feedback I am giving and receiving, and my expectation is the other party will do the same. Also, in taking responsibility, I always ensure when feedback is being given, I use non-inflammatory words, the feedback is given objectively, and most importantly, it is backed up by strong, demonstrative evidence. I'm not interested in hearsay.

If I am to give someone the courtesy of receiving feedback, the feedback must be worthy of being given. In my mind, it's not possible to give respectful feedback if the comments can't be backed up.

In approaching feedback this way, either in being the giver or receiver, there are three main lessons I have learned.

First: it's possible to have a deep and meaningful conversation and if done well, can strengthen the relationship even more. This was one piece of feedback I was given often by the teams I managed, and it resulted in our being friends outside of work, while I was their manager, and often for years after.

Second, it taught me on the receiving end, when I received feedback and reacted to it, that this was a sure sign I still had some healing and growing to do. An emotional reaction to feedback signals there is something within me I'm not owning, and it's out there, showing itself to the world. Time to look within, to be better.

Third and finally, and this is something I only learned recently: not all feedback, even when we are the recipient, is about us. It may be about the other.

If, when someone gives you feedback, you find you don't react, but there's a strong sense of, "I'm certain this is about you rather than me," don't be afraid to acknowledge this within yourself, and then find a way to either share this, or let it go.

People in pain often will not take responsibility or accountability for their actions, not own something within themselves they don't like, and may subconsciously project their failings onto you.

The first time this happened to me, I recall sitting there listening to feedback supposedly about me, and as the person talked I listened, and I was surprised when nothing within me reacted or felt the need to respond. I realised, as the person continued speaking, the person being described wasn't me, as I felt like I really knew me now.

At the end of the conversation it became clear this person was projecting her own foibles on me, and I knew no matter how I phrased it, she would never acknowledge this was about her. I thanked her for the feedback, shared my opinion by disagreeing, and asked for specific situations where I had behaved in this way so I could understand better. She struggled to answer this, and the conversation ended, whereby I asked if she ever had any concrete scenarios could she let me know, and I'd be more than willing to accept the feedback.

Therefore, having specific examples is critical. It allows the other a mirror to understand the context of the conversation and the subsequent impact and consequences.

One word of caution with the last point. Make sure you are absolutely, brutally honest with yourself that the feedback really isn't about you. Otherwise you too are projecting!

When you have clear principles about how to give and receive feedback, and you live and demonstrate this, it makes it much simpler to have conversations where your emotional strength serves you. You live and give the gift as the powerful, feminine leader you are.

251

Powerful Practice

Think about how you currently give and receive feedback in any aspect of your life, either personal or professional. How well does the process work for you?

Come up with your own principles about giving and receiving feedback from now on.

CHAPTER 55

Final Words—Owning Our Worth and Power, and Continuing the Journey

We're reaching the end of this journey and this book, and if I may, I'd like to share some parting thoughts.

As women, we may have been raised to play nice, be liked, and generally not rock the boat. There's nothing wrong with being nice or being liked, but being nice or liked at the cost of being whom we are, owning our worth, speaking up when needed, or whatever it is you've decided are your non-negotiables, and not rocking the boat is not an option. Not for me, anyway.

As women, I feel we put up with a lot of nonsense. This is I believe, because of the society we live in, is based on all I have talked about earlier. When we dare to be ourselves, speak up, question the status quo, or generally rock the boat, we may get called some terrible names.

Throughout my journey, I've learned there may be times when I must speak up and share what may not want to be heard. This is when, in the face of opposition (which can be mild to intense, and sometimes frightening) we as women must find ways of owning our worth and power, and being able to speak our truth. It may not always be received well, and we must be okay with this. It is a part of the journey.

This is what happens when we dare to live our lives our way. Not *the* way, as Wayne Dyer says. "There is no 'the' way. There is 'your' way, and there is 'my' way. 'The' way doesn't exist."

My final message is this. In owning our worth and power, there may be times when we will get called all sorts of names, either to our face, or behind our backs. Research shows that women who ask for what they want can be perceived negatively. It's time for this kind of nonsense to end and for us to keep stepping up and in and speaking out when needed. There is much happening in the world that needs our voices—the voices of the powerful, *divine* feminine in human form.

Our feminine power is very like the power of nature in all her glory. We have the power to create and destroy, and I believe it's time for the casting away and destruction of the harmful and often deadly influences and practices that strip away our feminine voice and power.

We must find the courage within us to be the women we dream of being, and stand up for what we believe to be true for us. In your journey forward, find the power and the voice to be the feminine leader you want to be and help end practices that keep women out of the spaces where we need to be. Now, more than ever.

I believe the true masculine energy of men is ready to work with the true feminine energy of women. It's not about one or the other. It's about both working together to create the visions we all have.

Blessed be.

Loving the journey; daring to play.

Regardless of what your beliefs may be when it comes to life, whether you believe in life after death or simply being worm food, right now, this life we're all living—this is the one we've got.

Our dreams exist because we exist, and because of the energy we send to them. Your dreams wait for you to help fashion them into reality, and right now, the only thing standing in the way of your dreams not happening is you.

I believe you hold and cherish your dreams deep within you, and through no fault of your own, when you've watched other dreams go out, or shrivel up and die, you've held onto the dreams still left even tighter.

I'm here to remind you of thing, and one thing only. You are the dream of the universe, and your dreams are the playground you came to play in.

They are waiting for you, and in awaiting you, they await all those who will be changed, because you dared play the game we all came to play, the only game there is.

The game of life and love.

Will you come out and play?

Be Her—Inside Out

There's only one rule to playing the game of life and love.

You must *be* her.

You know. The woman you decided you were, as you trawled through this book, and did all that was asked of you that I am deeply honoured you chose to be part of.

She is the dream waiting to be born, and she is the gift the world is waiting to receive.

In your having the courage and the love for yourself to ask for what you want, you shape the world and in the shaping, new desires and dreams are born, and the dream of you becomes much more than we could ever have imagined or dreamed.

In this final chapter, I have one final request to make of you, and as always, it's always your choice.

Will You Be Her?

Will you live and give your gift?

Will you help shape the world into what it dreams of being, ready for the future generations of females to come and experience what we have paved for them to live with every ounce of their being?

Will you *Be Her*?

I hope you say yes! With all your body, mind, heart, and soul.

As the journey has been.

Blessed be. Because we are.

.

EPILOGUE

Join the Movement

Dear Reader and Sister,

My dearest desire in writing this book was to create a resource that would allow women everywhere to have something to hand that would allow them to have the pesky money talk with their managers, without experiencing all we have discussed in this book.

Throughout my career, I have loved coaching and mentoring women, and this book was simply the next step for me in helping to get the message out.

I hope you've enjoyed the journey, received immense value, and are finding ways to implement all I have shared with you in your life. In the end, none of this matters if the knowledge isn't applied. For knowledge applied is wisdom, and my dearest hope is in your living and applying this knowledge and wisdom for yourself, you will consciously and subconsciously become the inspiration for women directly and indirectly in your sphere of influence.

It is in the sharing, applying, and emulating of what makes us better that makes the world better. The more women utilise this information, the more I see things like the pay gap become a thing of the past, and I know you think it's high time it was already gone!

Therefore, I have a couple of requests to make of you, and if you choose not to, I honour your decision.

First, if after reading, assimilating, and applying this information you ask for and receive what you want, please share your success with me at sabiha@highvaluewoman.org. I love hearing your stories, and they inspire me deeply to stay on this journey myself. For you and me.

Second, if this book has been of value to you, please share it with another. It is through conversations with likeminded women that we change ourselves, the paradigms we live in, and ultimately the world. Because in the end I can't do it without you. So, I ask for your help in making all of this happen, for all of us. Thank you from the bottom of my heart.

And if you'd like to continue your journey, come visit us at www.highvaluewoman.org and have a look around. You're welcome to stay as long as you like. Peruse the content, ask questions you need answers to, and if you'd like to stay in touch, simply join the "High Value Women's Club" and become part of the movement.

My vision is to help create a movement that empowers women to dream, create, and mould their future, especially when it comes to asking for what we want in our career and lives, and to help future generations of women to be and do the same. This way of being, I know will change the way women see themselves, and come to know intimately; *they* are the true wealth they seek, and always, in all ways, have been.

Thank you for being part of my journey and allowing me to be part of yours.

Blessed be,

Sabiha Vorajee